More Praise for *The Intelligent Optimist's Guide to Life*

"Every person in the world wants the same thing—to lead a happy, healthy, and fulfilling life. Yet most of us feel that ultimate goal is determined by external factors. In this fact-based, simple, and pragmatic book, Jurriaan Kamp shifts all the power into our own hands by illustrating that our view of the world around us is a self-fulfilling prophecy."
—**Bert Jacobs, cofounder and Chief Executive Optimist, The Life is good Company**

"Optimism is both the precondition and the precursor for individuals and organizations in making meaningful change, and Jurriaan Kamp does a wonderful job of reminding us just how powerful it can be."
—**Walter Robb, Co-CEO, Whole Foods Market**

"More and more research confirms that optimism is a critical ingredient of longevity and a healthy lifestyle. Jurriaan Kamp's book shows how you can improve your health through optimism."
—**Andrew Weil, MD**

"This book is like a good companion: it cheers you up."
—**Ben Knapen, former State Secretary for Foreign Affairs, The Netherlands**

"An inspired and inspiring guide to living with optimism in a world that is increasingly jaded and pessimistic—uplifting, rousing, and challenging us to dream the world into being in a positive and creative manner."
—**Alberto Villoldo, bestselling author of *Shaman, Healer, Sage***

"Optimism is a mindset, a lens through which to look at the world around us. It takes this mindset to be able to adapt to the changes that technology and climate change will bring our way. More importantly, this mindset also will give us the resolve to not just let change happen; we are the masters of our destiny and can shape a better world for all."
—**Peter Bakker, President, World Business Council for Sustainable Development**

"Thoughtfulness and inspiration are two ingredients that are mixed into a perspective that helps us look at the world as an optimist. There are many ways to journey through life, but the goal surely must be to live well. A good read and one you will want to pass on!"
—**Arkadi Kuhlmann, founder and CEO, ZenBanx**

"The world is full of opportunities for anyone wishing to see them. Media blur that vision and feed pessimism and depression. Optimism is in short supply. That should change and this book points the way."
—John Mackey, founder and Co-CEO, Whole Foods Market

"Pessimists, beware! This little book has the power to turn your mind around and, with it, your life! Rarely has the case for optimism been made with such precision and persuasion. The author has a genius for seeing deeply into the nature of our time and gives examples of how the world that seemingly isn't working actually is—and in a most elegant manner. To read this work is to cease giving credence to the whiny naysayers and instead to join the band of angels who carry a passion for the possible, advance the solutions, and engage in the creation of an emergent positive, practical, and successful world. Above all, it is fair to say that those readers who embrace the optimists' way will even stop boring God."
—Jean Houston, PhD, author of *The Wizard of Us*

"There's no problem in this world without a potential solution. What's too often lacking is the strategy to find these new solutions. That strategy is optimism—the desire to find the solution wherever it might be. It's the vital force for innovation in business and society. This is your handbook to create and contribute your solutions. Read and implement it!"
—Rinaldo Brutoco, entrepreneur and Founding President, World Business Academy

"This is a thought-provoking, challenging, and inspirational book. Jurriaan Kamp's unique way of looking at how we filter, use, and approach news and information is well worth considering. He is on a mission to help us all realign our thinking. Do yourself a favor and take the time to read and absorb *The Intelligent Optimist's Guide to Life*."
—Robert J. Rosenthal, Executive Director, The Center for Investigative Reporting

"Jurriaan is just the kind of visionary we need today: well-informed, pragmatic, and indefatigably optimistic. His lively book should wake up readers who are using their pessimism as an excuse for inactivity."
—Bryan Welch, Publisher and Editorial Director, Ogden Publications, and General Manager, Capper's Insurance Service, Inc.

THE INTELLIGENT OPTIMIST'S GUIDE TO LIFE

THE INTELLIGENT OPTIMIST'S GUIDE TO LIFE

How to Find Health and Success in a World That's a Better Place Than You Think

Jurriaan Kamp

BK

Berrett–Koehler Publishers, Inc.
San Francisco
a BK Life book

Berrett-Koehler Publishers, Inc.
235 Montgomery Street, Suite 650
San Francisco, CA 94104-2916
Tel: (415) 288-0260   Fax: (415) 362-2512   www.bkconnection.com

Ordering Information

Quantity sales. Special discounts are available on quantity purchases by corporations, associations, and others. For details, contact the "Special Sales Department" at the Berrett-Koehler address above.

Individual sales. Berrett-Koehler publications are available through most bookstores. They can also be ordered directly from Berrett-Koehler: Tel: (800) 929-2929; Fax: (802) 864-7626; www.bkconnection.com

Orders for college textbook/course adoption use. Please contact Berrett-Koehler: Tel: (800) 929-2929; Fax: (802) 864-7626.

Orders by U.S. trade bookstores and wholesalers. Please contact Ingram Publisher Services, Tel: (800) 509-4887; Fax: (800) 838-1149; E-mail: customer.service@ingrampublisherservices.com; or visit www.ingrampublisherservices.com/Ordering for details about electronic ordering.

Berrett-Koehler and the BK logo are registered trademarks of Berrett-Koehler Publishers, Inc.

Printed in Canada

Berrett-Koehler books are printed on long-lasting acid-free paper. When it is available, we choose paper that has been manufactured by environmentally responsible processes. These may include using trees grown in sustainable forests, incorporating recycled paper, minimizing chlorine in bleaching, or recycling the energy produced at the paper mill.

Library of Congress Cataloging-in-Publication Data

Kamp, Jurriaan.
The intelligent optimist's guide to life : how to find health and success in a world that's a better place than you think / Jurriaan Kamp.
-- First Edition.
     pages cm
Includes bibliographical references and index.
ISBN 978-1-62656-275-2 (pbk.)
1. Optimism. I. Title.
BF698.35.O57K36 2014
149'.5--dc23
                                  2014021172

First Edition
19 18 17 16 15 14   10 9 8 7 6 5 4 3 2 1

Interior design: Laura Lind Design   *Editor:* Pam Suwinsky
Cover design: Carl de Vaal   *Proofreader:* Henri Bensussen
Horseman image: Ruediger Dahlke   *Indexer:* Do Mi Stauber
Production service: Linda Jupiter Productions

To Hélène, the love of my life and the better optimist

No pessimist ever discovered the secret of the stars, or sailed an uncharted land or opened a new doorway for the human spirit.

—*Helen Keller*

CONTENTS

A NOTE FROM THE AUTHOR

One of the privileges of being a reporter is that it is your job to always look for new stories and thus you always meet new people.

Through all these meetings over many years I have learned that a lot of people choose vocations that they themselves can learn the most from.

Many psychotherapists have a great need to heal their own psyches.

Mediators tend to create conflicts in their personal lives.

High-energy motivational speakers who talk about the power of positive thinking appear to ignore the negative in their own lives.

Business gurus who teach that egos are so often roadblocks in business have big egos themselves.

People who teach meditation and mindfulness tend to need to quiet their own minds.

It is like healing your own wounds becomes the most important and inspiring contribution you can make to the world around you.

Then there are also the people who are natural teachers. They don't need to write books or tell their stories to big audiences. They just *are*. And through their beings they teach and inspire. Talking or writing about something is different from *being* that same thing. From being flows natural inspiration. No need for books or talks.

So where does that leave me as the maker of a magazine and a book on optimism?

Am I a pessimist who himself needs more optimism?

Someone once asked me, "How could you construct doors without locks and windows without shades if you don't know the power of the negative?"

So, yes, I was born an optimist—like you, for that matter. But—probably like you too—I have encountered disappointments early in life that weakened my natural ability to remain optimistic. At some point I made it my mission to overcome my disappointments and the pessimism that came from it.

Many people never need to read a book on optimism because they already are optimists. That is to say their optimism is stronger than their pessimism. It is important to recognize that in our dualistic world all of us are both optimists and pessimists. The fact is that our lives are more fulfilling as optimists than as pessimists. Science is very clear about that, as you will read in this book.

I know from my own experience that pessimists can become optimists, and that the journey from pessimism to optimism is a very rewarding one. At the same time many optimists can strengthen their optimism. Perhaps, because I do know the pessimistic parts in me as well as the optimistic parts I can be a good guide for you on the road to more optimism.

I look forward to sharing what I've learned with you, as well as many stories that have inspired me. I wrote this book to motivate and energize you and to inspire you to live your life to the fullest.

That's optimism. And this is your guide.

STORIES, NEWS, AND THE CHALLENGE OF OPTIMISM

Media distort reality and breed pessimism. We need
optimism for more health, happiness, and success.
We need freedom *from* the press to get there.

IN THE BEGINNING
WAS THE STORY

We create our reality through our stories.

Every change begins with a story.

Societies rise and fall by the stories they tell.

Our lives are made by the stories we hear and the ones we tell ourselves.

That's why media—as our professional storytellers—play such an important role.

That's why it matters that media focus almost exclusively on whatever goes wrong.

Media feed pessimism and depression.

Media stand in the way of solutions that could help improve lives and our world at large.

And that's why a book on optimism has to start with a story about the news.

MORE BOMBS,
MORE MONEY

I spent the first ten years of my career as a reporter at the leading newspaper in my country, the Netherlands. I worked in the newsroom in Rotterdam before becoming a correspondent in Delhi, India, and ultimately leading the economics desk. In chasing news, I came to a deep understanding of something we all know: Media are much more interested in what goes wrong than in what goes right. If it bleeds, it leads. In India, on a freelance contract, more bombs meant more monthly revenue for me.

I used to think the negative, pessimistic focus of the media was grounded in the choices of the writers and editors. I thought that if the writers changed the way they saw the world, we would have more balanced newspapers and broadcasts.

As much as I still support that perspective, I now know things are much more complicated. It's not just that many of my former colleagues were pessimists, always suspicious, and preferred dressing in black.

The press is under siege.

It all comes from a big misunderstanding. Somehow, somewhere, in the decades since World War II, we have started confusing telling stories—informing the public—with selling watches, cars, soda, and toothbrushes.

Nowadays, publishers are supposed to target certain well-defined interest groups. In fact, each new media initiative starts by defining its audience. As much sense as that seems to make in today's money-driven world, it's unethical. Media's contribution should come from their stories, their content—not their capacity to serve a certain audience and to attract money from advertisers. There is, I'm afraid, more policy behind the ads or commercials than behind the stories. With small exceptions here and there, there's no free press anymore. But standing in the way of this crucial constitutional right is not a dictator—it's the market economy. It's capitalism.

"History has shown that competition and free markets deliver real value . . . something we should encourage," Rupert Murdoch said when he acquired the *Wall Street Journal* in 2007. This may be true in many industries. Better cars drive on India's roads today than they did twenty-five years ago, when the Indian economy was basically closed. But the same model has not led to better journalism. It won't lead to better symphony orchestras either. We have to save certain parts of our society from the thinking of the Rupert Murdochs.

THE EROSION OF DEMOCRACY

Watergate is a heroic example of the importance of the free press. But do you remember how long it took for media to start questioning America's invasion of Iraq? Numbed by the terrorist attacks of September 11, 2001, it took some two years before important critical questions about weapons of mass destruction and more were raised in the media. The American people were deceived—much like at the time of Watergate—because the media were not leading the quest for the truth.

And do you remember that Disney refused to distribute Michael Moore's *Fahrenheit 9/11* because, as Disney executives said, "It's not in the interest of any major corporation to be dragged into a highly charged partisan political battle."

Would that be language Katherine Graham, the publisher of the *Washington Post* in the Watergate era, would ever have used?

The problem is that Disney is in the wrong position to begin with. Disney is an entertainment company. Such a company has nothing to do with serving the freedom of the press. But Disney has become one of a handful of big corporations that own most of the media in the United States. These corporations increasingly sell "infotainment"—a word that reveals why Kim Kardashian and Paris Hilton frequent the pages and websites of serious media.

In the meantime, the fourth pillar of democracy is staggering.

I'VE MADE BOOKCASES, BUT I'M NOT A CARPENTER

The press doesn't matter anymore, some will argue. We have Twitter. News spreads instantly through social media. These days, we are all journalists.

The evolution of social media certainly brings a lot of good. Whereas the average front page is 90 percent frauds, floods, fires, murders, and diseases, research shows that what people share on social media is more positive than negative. The more positive an article, the more likely it's going to be shared, explains Jonah Berger, social psychologist at the University of Pennsylvania, in his book *Why Things Catch On.* And in an interview with the *New York Times* he said, "The 'If it bleeds' rule works for mass media that just want you to tune in. They want your eyeballs and don't care how you're feeling. But when you share a story with your friends and peers, you care a lot more how they react. You don't want them to think of you as a Debbie Downer."[1]

So friends care about each other, and tweeting and sharing tend to be more positive. But tweeting is no journalism. Journalists are trained for years to write good news stories that cover all relevant angles. Good journalism is a trade. It should present and explain the news. It should investigate and discover. Media should always be on a quest for the truth. Social media should complement that, not replace it.

Let me put it like this: I've made bookcases for our home. Recently, we hired a carpenter to do the same. I could easily see the difference between his work and mine. I'm definitely not a carpenter.

OBJECTIVITY AND TOOTHBRUSHES

Leading media pride themselves on objectivity and fairness. They follow a strict policy of fair reporting that includes the facts and perspectives of all the interested parties. But I'd like to put this objectivity to the test. If you ask the people you meet today how their day is going, most people will say that in their lives more is going right than wrong. Yes, all of us suffer from pain and loss from time to time. But it's fair to say that in most lives most of the time more goes right than wrong. Ultimately, our world is quite a happy place (more about that later).

Now imagine a visitor from outer space who just reads the papers and watches television news to get an idea about this newfound world. Without meeting with real people, that visitor will think this is a place of despair and failure. Media are not objective. Far from it. Media distort and misrepresent our reality.

While I was reporting in Afghanistan in the late 1980s, I saw with my own eyes that journalists were "adjusting" stories to meet the expectations of their newsrooms. If the *mujahideen* resistance fighters were quiet that day, they were made to be dangerous. They had to be to make sure newsstand sales didn't plummet. It was never official policy, but the pressure to "perform" was always in the air. Evelyn Waugh wrote a satirical novel about this: *Scoop*. I only wish reality was not so close to his satire.

Media use a tool dictators have used with great success for centuries. They spread fear and pessimism because it sells. Editorial choices are determined by business interests and by stock prices. Newspapers have become like toothbrushes. Stories have become commercials.

GREAT INNOVATION . . . ONE PROBLEM

I remember when the paper came in the morning. In the evening, we watched the news. In between: no news. That changed during the first Gulf War in 1991, when CNN jumped on the scene with twenty-four-hour broadcasting. Great innovation . . . one problem: There was not enough news—or so it seemed, because the same stories kept being repeated again and again, hour after hour.

In the past, the onslaught of negativity was restricted to twice a day. Now it has become a twenty-four-hour bombardment that continues in elevators, at gas stations, and in bars where people meet to relax.

It matters which stories we tell each other. If media continually shout that the world is falling apart, we will register that and it will influence our perspectives. It's much harder to see a beautiful world when you get reports only about problems and disasters.

Between 1990—one year before the twenty-four-hour news invention—and 2010, the world population grew 40 percent—mostly in developing countries. According to the World Health Organization (WHO), the number of people suffering from depression rose 300 percent—mostly in rich countries—making it one of the biggest challenges to health and well-being. I'm not a social scientist, but I see a remarkable correlation between the rise of depression and pessimism and the twenty-four-hour negative news invasion over the same twenty-year period.

HOW DO YOU FEED YOUR MIND?

In recent decades, many of us have discovered that what we eat makes a big difference to our health. We have changed our diets. We take better care of our bodies.

But most people still don't pay much attention to how they feed their minds. And the impact of what we put in our eyes and ears is as deep as what we put in our mouths. "News is to the mind what sugar is to the body. News is easy to digest," wrote Rolf Dobelli in the *Guardian*.[2]

To be healthy, we need to avoid sugar. It's the same with the news. Like bad eating habits, continuous exposure to bad news makes you sick.

What makes it worse is that the news is often irrelevant to you. *Black Swan* author Nassim Taleb gives a good example. When a big bridge collapses, the "news" interest will be on the person in the last truck that made it over. That may be sensational but it's not relevant to you. What is relevant is the story about the fragility of the bridge. Was it a structural problem? Could that happen in a similar bridge you go over one day?

News is often about things you cannot influence. What can you do about the next bomb blast in Afghanistan? Or even about the next tortured and twisted soul who opens fire on an innocent school crowd? Nothing. But these sad stories do make you feel powerless and helpless. That's how the news feeds pessimism and depression.

It's a fair guess that you read some twenty-four news stories every day, or at least their headlines. That comes to some 10,000 news stories per year. Do you remember a story you read in the past year that has helped you make a better decision about your life? Most news is not helpful to you. It interrupts your thinking. It stands in the way of creativity and the emergence of new ideas. As Rolf Dobelli wrote in the *Guardian*, "If you want to come up with old solutions, read news. If you are looking for new solutions, don't."[3]

So often what is presented as *news* is really *olds*. It is not about innovation, breakthroughs, solutions, or new insights. In short, it's not optimistic. It's about sad repetitions of unfortunate events that don't support and enrich your life. That's very pessimistic.

FREEDOM *FROM* THE PRESS

We are always calling on developing countries to allow for freedom *of* the press. But the Western world faces something as important: We need freedom *from* the press. Freedom from a press that focuses on negative news to the exclusion of the good. Freedom from a press run by advertisers rather than by journalists. Freedom from a press in which the bottom line is more important than the common good. And—most important—freedom from a press that feeds depression and pessimism and stands in the way of progress.

TWO FREE WEEKS AND MORE HAPPINESS

If you are like most people, you spend an hour a day watching or reading the news.

Research has shown that after watching the news for fifteen minutes, most people need fifteen minutes of relaxation exercises to get rid of the resulting anxiety and mood disturbances. (Don't think you aren't one of them. The research shows that the news affects *everyone*.)[4]

I don't know anyone who does that. But more important, why would you consume the anxiety-provoking news in the first place? That's a very poor investment of your time.

Imagine what you could do with your time if you stopped reading and watching the news. One hour a day equals fifteen full days a year that you could invest in activities that give meaning to your life.

"Another press is possible." That slogan was on our T-shirts when we launched the English-language edition of our magazine at the World Social Forum in Porte Alegre, Brazil, in early 2003. It is a T-shirt I often wear. We want to live in a different world. A healthier, greener, happier, and more just world. For that world to become reality, we need more optimism and different stories. The press should find these stories. But, ultimately, these stories begin with you and me. When you embrace optimism and take the time to discover your story, your life will become richer and happier and the world will be a better place.

chapter 1

THE BEST WAY
TO LIVE

Pessimism and optimism are strategies. We create
pessimism as a response to what happens to us.
But we can also respond with optimism to the
events in our life. And that's much more rewarding.

BAD WEATHER AND UNFOUNDED OPTIMISM

In high school, my week revolved around the field hockey game on Saturday. Back then, we still played on real grass. Hence, as the week progressed, a striking parallel arose between my mood and darkening skies. Too much rain would force the game to be canceled, which routinely happened in the fall and winter. My grumbling started well in advance. If it were raining cats and dogs on a Friday afternoon, my dear mother would try to cheer me up by looking out the window and pointing at a random piece of sky. "Look," she'd exclaim, "it's already clearing up over there!"

That unfounded optimism always infuriated me.

Yet she had a point. After the rain there will always be sunshine. Yes, bad things happen. But it is our choice to accept the rain and look beyond it to the coming sunshine. We create pessimism by our focus on the bad. At the same time we create optimism by focusing on the good. And, as we shall see, optimism is a much more rewarding strategy.

Optimism doesn't mean denying reality. According to the dictionary, the everyday meaning of *optimism* is "hopefulness and confidence about the future or the success of something." But the root of the word comes from Latin (*optimum*) and the more precise definition of optimism is "the doctrine that this world is the best of all possible worlds."

Optimism is a fundamental attitude. It's not an opinion about reality; it's a starting point for dealing with reality. At every moment, you can decide that you're in the best situation to handle a given challenge. *That* is optimism. Optimism is searching for the *yes* in every situation and finding it. Or as someone once aptly described that attitude: "If there's no solution, then there's no problem."

PESSIMISM: A GIGANTIC ROADBLOCK

"This pessimism is lying across modern civilization like some enormous fallen tree and somehow we've got to get a bulldozer and shift it out of the way," said the English writer and "the first philosopher of optimism in European history" Colin Wilson.[1]

According to Wilson, the roots of the pessimism epidemic go back to the Romantics of the early nineteenth century whose message was that humans could only briefly experience "exquisite happiness," but it was not meant to be forever and life was supposed to be miserable. "Most people still don't understand what has happened in Western culture over the past two centuries. How the long defeatist curve that originated in the early 19th century continues to cloud our way of thinking," said Wilson.

Human beings have a unique capacity to find new answers through the expansion of their consciousness. That's why optimism, the art of finding solutions, is a more logical way of life than the, in intellectual circles, still dominant—pessimistic—worldview that was "invented" by a few poets 200 years ago.

Life will inevitably deal us some bad hands from time to time. Life is not simple. That it should be is a contemporary misconception fed by modern consumerism, which offers a quick solution for every inconvenience. An increasing stream of gurus have extrapolated from that material prosperity to claim that life can be, should be, an effortless affair.

All those messages seem to have made us less of a match for life. Our ancestors trekked across the steppes and savannas. They knew they were continually in danger. They didn't know life could be anything *but* challenging. Our reality consists of hospitals, insurance policies, and benefit payments when things go wrong. The welfare state has strongly influenced our expectations, but it still doesn't preclude bad things from happening.

In 1978, psychiatrist M. Scott Peck wrote *The Road Less Traveled*. The book begins like this: "Life is difficult. This is a great truth, one of the greatest truths. It is a great truth because once we truly see this truth, we transcend it. Once we truly know that life is difficult—once we truly understand and accept it—then life is no longer difficult. Because once it is accepted, the fact that life is difficult no longer matters."

Every religion and philosophy of life teaches that the meaning of life lies in our responses to the challenges we encounter. Our life lessons are the essence of our existence. That's why the way we face those lessons is so important. "Pain is inevitable, suffering is optional," Buddhists say. Optimism turns out to be the most promising and fulfilling strategy, because the optimist accepts reality and then *does* something about it.

RESILIENCE IS MORE USEFUL THAN SUSTAINABILITY

In more and more environmental dialogues the word *resilience* begins to replace the word *sustainability*. Sustainability means keeping things intact. It means avoiding causing damage. It's about preventing change. Sustainability is a static concept.

Resilience, though, is dynamic. "The capacity to recover quickly from difficulties," says one definition. Resilience is part of ongoing change. The world today is not the same as the world of 5,000 years ago. Nor will the world of the future much resemble our current reality. That's why sustainability is not a helpful concept in a world of continual and rapid change.

The same applies to our daily lives. They will never be sustainable in the static sense. We can only frustrate ourselves by not accepting the changes we cannot escape. That frustration is at the root of much pessimism. The optimist is resilient. She evolves with circumstances and times.

Bad days will come. But the point is, they will go as well. So the challenge is to go as untouched as possible through the bad days. That's where resilience comes in. But *untouched* does not mean "disconnected." Resilience means remaining part of the circumstances and adapting, taking the fact in, learning the lesson—understanding and accepting—and moving on.

The focus of the optimist is on the potential change. She embraces *yes* and fights against *no*. The optimist makes the conscious choice to endure in times of hardship. It is illuminating that the Chinese use the same character for *endurance* as for *patience*: the patience required to wait for the moment when you can once again act effectively. That wise patience is also evident in theologian Reinhold Niebuhr's famous prayer: "Grant me the serenity to accept the things I cannot change, the courage to change the things I can, and the wisdom to know the difference."

Optimism, persistence, and resilience go hand in hand. You can't find answers or solutions if you aren't prepared to keep searching and digging. At the same time, you can't find them if you don't first accept the truth at the deepest level. That's often a painful process. Optimism isn't always fun and happy.

You don't want to sustain your life as it is; you want it to be resilient and adaptable to the ever-ongoing change around you.

THERE IS NO BAD WEATHER, ONLY INAPPROPRIATE CLOTHING

Boston Philharmonic conductor Benjamin Zander and his former wife psychotherapist Rosamund Stone Zander wrote a bestselling book: *The Art of Possibility*. It is an art that every optimist has to master. Zander precisely distinguishes living in possibility from aiming for the possible, or hoping, or positive thinking:

"The possible is what you can achieve. Politics is the art of the possible. Possibility is not hope either. Hope comes from not being able to deal with the present. It is not positive thinking. I hate that. You can always tell that positive thinkers don't want to deal with the negative. It is not possibilities, plural. That's about our options, our choices. Possibility, however, is a domain. In every experience there is possibility. It is available to us every moment of the day. It is about one choice: To be in the present, and . . . "[2]

. . . and in that moment the future can unfold and the answer can come.

Zander's penchant for possibility started early. He speaks passionately about his father, who inspired his children with a Scandinavian proverb: "There is no such thing as bad weather, only inappropriate clothing."

"Possibility is a place of imagination and response. Human beings have a capacity to accept and react. To say: Great! What's next?," says Zander.

We suffer a lot of unnecessary pain because we don't say, "Great! What's next?" We don't respond, and we judge too early. Zhou Enlai, the Chinese leader, was asked in the early 1970s about the impact of the French Revolution. "Too early to tell," Zhou Enlai is supposed to have answered.

Zhou likely misunderstood his interpreter. However, the anecdote points to an important message. If we are really smart when something happens to us, we won't immediately judge and say it's good or bad. So often a painful loss opens the door to a new and deeply meaningful experience that could not have happened without the preceding loss. The circle of life requires a rigorous discipline to stay in the state of mind of possibility and resilience. It is indeed too early to tell.

SCHOOLS BREED PESSIMISTS

In studies on happiness, the French consistently rack up the lowest scores in the Western world. The material quality of their lives is comparable to that of people in neighboring countries. Measured over long time periods, French economic growth is consistent with European averages. Yet the French are more pessimistic. Far more than other Europeans, they expect their lives to get worse, and they are the top consumers of antidepressants. Why is that?

Writing in the *Financial Times*, Claudia Senik, a professor of economics at the Sorbonne in Paris, indicated a possible source of French pessimism: the educational system. The French system assumes all students will achieve the same top outcome. In reality, of course, they cannot all enjoy the finest educations at the best universities. As a result, the system undermines the self-confidence of French teenagers, according to Senik. High school students feel powerless.

Powerlessness is the root of pessimism. We are all born optimists. Who has ever met a pessimistic four-year-old? A child who fell on the playground and, after having her tears dried and the scratch on her knee bandaged, decided never to run again? Those children don't exist. Children get up, try again, and keep laughing, even through their tears. Every child has the instinctive intelligence to keep trying. Young children don't feel powerless.

A lot of optimism gets lost in high school, and not just in France. Expectations increase. Exams and grades multiply. This creates a hierarchy within which the student is judged. No one used to count who had the bloodiest knees; suddenly, failing grades are tallied. The system strongly implies that people with higher grades lead better, more successful lives. That is an illusion of control. Those with poor scores have less control; they are more powerless; and they become more pessimistic. Education is supposed to be about opening children's hearts and minds to new experiences. However, grades stand in the way. The educational system is a devastating experience for many children. It is a factory that produces pessimists.

WE NEED VICTORIES— VICTORIES FOR ALL

Like pessimism, optimism can be created. And we do so through our victories. There's plenty of research that shows that we need victories in our lives. Success is good for us. Success gives us energy. Defeat takes energy away. But if we judge too early, we may misjudge an event as a defeat. Later on it may turn out to be a victory. Many athletes say that they had to endure difficult losses to build the strength to become great champions. At the same time we sometimes need to keep losing to make us see that we need to radically change a direction in our life—that our victory lies somewhere else.

After breaking his legs three times within two years, one of Germany's most promising young skiers was forced to quit his favorite sport. Because he did, he went to medical school and became a doctor who discovered a new, innovative healing therapy. His "failure" at skiing bred his success as a doctor. Looking back, he's grateful that he missed the medals but found the mission that fulfills his life. With his broken legs he felt a loser. Now, looking back, he feels a victor.

Optimism is not a zero-sum game. Optimism just produces *life*, ever more life. The optimist is not the winner in the traditional sense. The optimist is not the one who defeats the pessimist. Optimism has nothing to do with the culture of competition that so deeply undermines modern society. There's a big difference between competing at the expense of another and overcoming challenges that make you a wiser, more loving, more compassionate, and more whole human being. The battle is with yourself, not with the other. The optimist is the winner in that personal battle. And her hard-fought victory of resilience, her gain of wisdom and understanding is a victory for all.

In the game of life, all of us can be victors. No one is destined to only lose in life. And we need much more of such victories in our interconnected world where failure in one country—or even of one company—can bring down the entire global system. We have entered a world where we can flourish only if we all win. That united winning requires the discipline of optimism. The more of us who commit to their personal victories, the more of us will benefit. Optimism is a strategy that enhances life and serves us all.

RESPONSE-ABILITY

The word responsibility can be neatly parsed: *response-ability*, the ability to provide a response. That ability forms the core of the optimistic lifestyle. Back to the stumbling preschooler: We don't fail when we fall; we fail when we don't get back up. Getting back up, one way or another, is always an option. That's response-ability.

The most striking example of this vision is the book *Man's Search for Meaning* by Austrian psychiatrist Viktor Frankl. Frankl wrote the book in the days after he was freed from a concentration camp in 1945. The original German title reveals more about the book's message. *Trotzdem Ja zum Leben sagen* means "yes to life despite everything." When Frankl was sent to the concentration camp, he decided to put his psychiatric training to the ultimate test: How does the human mind work in extremely challenging, dehumanizing circumstances? He observed what kept some people going and what pulled the rug out from under others and wrote, "Everything can be taken from a man but one thing, the last of the human freedoms: to choose one's attitude in any given set of circumstances, to choose one's own way."

The optimist knows he is not in control of all that happens in his life, but that he does determine his response to it. The pessimist feels like a victim; the optimist searches for solutions.

And there is always a solution, or at least the beginning of one. After actor Michael J. Fox developed Parkinson's disease, he related in a television interview how he finally came to terms with it: "The answer had nothing to do with protection and everything to do with perspective. The only choice not available to me was whether or not I had Parkinson's. Everything else was up to me. I could concentrate on what I'd lost, or I could keep living and discover how the holes would fill themselves back up."

WHY IS THE BEGINNING OF *HOW*

Optimism and decisiveness also go hand in hand. Optimists act. That's why entrepreneurs are optimists. "Optimism is an essential condition for doing something difficult," says Jeff Bezos, the founder of Amazon.com. By acting, by doing something, you enter into relationship with the reality around you. That makes *the* reality *your* reality. And that gives meaning to your life. That kind of meaning is missing in many lives today.

Long ago, you were born on a farm and you were needed to help in the fields and in the stables. You knew what your life would look like and what you would do. That clarity provided something to hold onto. Today, everyone can be everything, but that is the flip side of everything is nothing. Many lives strand in that abyss. As the philosopher Friedrich

Nietzsche said, "He who has a *why* to live for can bear with almost any *how*."

Advertisements sell the good life after sixty-five when you can live off your savings—if properly invested with the advertising company, of course. But what is often overlooked is that neither "getting paid to sit at home" nor going on frequent vacations provides you with a fulfilling sense of purpose. You're better off doing something than having "free time."

In 2006, San Francisco commemorated the major earthquake of 1906. The *San Francisco Chronicle* ran a story about a 106-year-old man who had lived through the earthquake as a boy. He described that experience, but he also talked about his current life. Every day, he got up at six in the morning to go to work, stocking the shelves at the grocery store a few blocks from his house. He still enjoyed his job. He belonged somewhere. He had a purpose.

THERE'S ALWAYS A WAY

Optimists naturally embrace two elements more readily than pessimists. Optimists are grateful, and they have a sense of humor. They take themselves less seriously. "Laughter is the currency of hope," Frankl said. Norman Cousins, American political journalist, author, and professor of medical humanities, overcame a painful disease by watching Marx Brothers films. "Laughter interrupts the panic cycle of an illness," he wrote in his autobiography, *Anatomy of an Illness*. There is a correlation between laughter and the levels of certain hormones in the body that regulate our perception of pain. Who hasn't experienced laughter as a welcome balm in the middle of grief and misery? It's as if the painful reality fades for a time, and space opens up for a new and broader perspective.

There will always be problems. That won't ever change. What you can change is the way you approach those problems: with gratitude for the chance to learn a new lesson, gratitude for the opportunity to find a path that may provide new fulfillment, and thanks for everything that is working and for everything that makes your life good. That gratitude is the converse of the pessimist's disappointment.

The Brazilians have a saying that might explain why they always place near the top in the list of most optimistic countries. *Da um jeitinho*: There's always a way. It's true. And because that way exists, my mother was right after all: Dark skies are always clearing up. That's why optimism offers us the best way to live.

chapter 2

A KEY TO HEALTH, HAPPINESS, AND SUCCESS

An overview of the compelling research that shows
that optimism supports your health and happiness
and leads to success.

LEARNED HELPLESSNESS

The research into the impact of an optimistic lifestyle on the health of an individual began with American psychologist Martin Seligman. Seligman started his career at the University of Pennsylvania in clinical psychology by doing what many others had done before him. He began looking for what was wrong with people and would try to fix it. Psychology subscribed to the disease model of human functioning, with the main purpose of intervention being to repair damage. The general perspective on health is the same: Health is the absence of illness. We talk about *health* care policies, but in reality we are dealing with *disease* policies. In the same way, within Seligman's world, mental health merely meant the absence of mental illness.

Early in his career, to get a better understanding about the impact of this focus on the negative side of life, Seligman pursued research with his partners Steve Maier and Bruce Overmier that would lead them to the discovery of "learned helplessness."

The three scientists found that rats and mice in labs became passive and gave up in the face of adversity after they experienced negative events they could do nothing about. Their first experience with helplessness—a mildly painful shock they could not avoid—made them passive, and they gave up any attempt to escape. Other animals that had experienced the same physical shock but could escape it did not become helpless and passive. The ability to escape "immunized" against learned helplessness.

In a further experiment, Seligman and his students implanted a tumor with a 50 percent lethality rate on the flanks of rats. Subsequently, these rats were divided into three groups: One group went through a series of mildly painful escapable shocks; one group went through an identical series of inescapable shocks; and a control group experienced no shock at all.

As expected, 50 percent of the rats in the control group that had not experienced any shock died. Seventy-five percent of the rats in the "inescapable" group died—illustrating that helplessness weakened the body. And 25 percent of the rats in the "escapable" group died—demonstrating that control over life strengthens the body.[1]

Seligman had proven that benevolent events strengthen the immune system. He had laid the foundation for optimism as a strategy for better health. The general focus in health care on repairing damage does only half the job: It corrects deficits but fails to build strength.

OPTIMISM PROTECTS AGAINST HEART DISEASE AND CANCER

The case for optimism as a driver for health and happiness was born. To test their premise, Seligman and his team got involved with a study of 120 men from San Francisco who had had their first heart attacks. Psychologists and cardiologists were trying to prove that training the men to change their personalities from aggressive and hostile to easygoing would have an impact on their heart disease. It didn't.

But subsequently Seligman and his team used the extensive interviews with the men to rate their optimism, counting the "because" statements that showed how they explained whatever happened to them in their lives (see chapter 4). Within eight and a half years, half the men had died of a second heart attack. Could Seligman predict who would have a second heart attack? As Seligman writes in his book *Flourish*, none of the usual risk factors predicted death: not blood pressure, not cholesterol, not how extensive the damage from the first heart attack was. Only the men's levels of optimism eight and a half years earlier predicted the second heart attack. Of the sixteen most pessimistic men, fifteen died. Of the sixteen most optimistic men, only five died.[2]

This finding has been confirmed in many studies since. One landmark study was done in The Netherlands. Nine hundred and ninety-nine 65- to 85-year-olds were followed for nine years. At the beginning of the study in 1991, all participants had to answer the following four questions on a 1 to 3 scale.

1. I still expect much from life.

2. I do not look forward to what lies ahead for me in the years to come.

3. I am still full of plans.

4. I often feel that life is full of promises.

During the nine years of the study, 397 subjects died. Pessimism was very strongly associated with mortality. Optimists experienced only 23 percent of the heart disease deaths of pessimists, and only 55 percent of the overall death rate compared to the pessimists.[3]

The relationship among optimism, pessimism, and heart disease goes two ways in the studies. High optimists die at a lower rate and high pessimists die at a higher rate than average. Optimism strengthens people against heart disease, just as pessimism weakens them.

Does optimism deliver a better outcome in the case of cancer as well? The research is less clear because the optimism advantage seems to relate most to the functioning of the immune system. That system is critical to protecting against the onset of cancer—and that's where optimism provides a key protection advantage—but once cancer is diagnosed, many other factors (the endocrine system, the autonomous nervous system) begin playing a role too, and the optimism factor diminishes.

In *Flourish*, Seligman cites the most complete review of the link between optimism and cancer in the meta-study "Optimism and Physical Health."[4] This study analyzes eighty-three separate studies of optimism and physical health; eighteen of these, involving 2,858 patients, concern cancer. Seligman writes, "Taken together, they find that more optimistic people have better cancer outcomes at a robust level of significance," and he concludes, "My overview of the cancer literature is that it leans heavily in the direction of pessimism as a risk factor for developing cancer."

OPTIMISM BOOSTS THE IMMUNE SYSTEM

Many studies show that optimism is good for your health. Optimistic mothers give birth to bigger and healthier babies.[5] Optimists recover more quickly from disease and surgery.[6] Optimists live longer.[7] But how optimism does that is less clear. That's why Suzanne Segerstrom, professor of psychology at the University of Kentucky, has been researching the relationship between optimism and the immune system for many years. In one of her most recent studies she worked with a group of 124 first-year law students. The students were studied five times over six months. Each time, they answered questions about how optimistic they felt about law school. Then they were injected with material that should summon an immune response. Two days later, they came back to have the injection site measured. A larger bump in the skin meant a stronger immune response.

The study gave an outcome that confirms earlier findings by Segerstrom.[8] A general optimistic outlook on life does not necessarily lead to differences in immune responses among students. But what does make a difference is optimism linked to specific events, like, in Segerstrom's study, grades and tests results. As each student's expectations about law school waxed and waned, their immune response followed along. At more optimistic times, they'd have bigger immune responses; at a more pessimistic time, more sluggish immune responses.

So, being optimistic about success in a specific, important domain promotes better immunity. Simply put: If your grades give you confidence that you are a good law student, you tend to be optimistic about your next tests. And with this optimism comes a stronger immune system. A little optimism helps. Segerstrom: "If people have slightly more positive views of the future than is actually true, that's adaptive."

OPTIMISM IS A CURE FOR DEPRESSION

The research is abundant and clear: Optimism is good for your physical health. But what about your mental health? Specifically, is there a link to the depression epidemic that infests many countries in the Western world? Compared to the history of our ancestors, we live in the best possible times (see chapter 5). There's more peace; we are in better health; we live longer with a higher standard of living. Yet we are more depressed. There's more pessimism than ever. And so the question is, Can we fight the depression epidemic by spreading optimism?

Pessimism and depression are linked. Martin Seligman gave questionnaires to thousands of depressed people and consistently found that they were also pessimistic. However, that does not necessarily mean pessimism causes depression. In a multiyear study, Seligman found that pessimistic children are more likely to become and stay depressed. But that may merely indicate that pessimism precedes and predicts depression rather than causing it.

Then he followed a different reasoning: If pessimism were the cause of depression, changing pessimism into optimism should relieve the depression. Seligman knew that it was possible to teach pessimists to become optimists (see chapter 4). In a study of depressed pessimists, subjects were taught through cognitive therapy to change the way they explain life events to themselves (their "explanatory style"; see chapter 4).[9] The study showed that changing explanatory style from pessimism to optimism relieves depression markedly.

Changing the way people think about their lives turned out to be far more effective in relieving depression than dispensing drugs. It also means optimism is indeed a cure for depression. Pessimism is not the only cause of depression (genes, hormones, and other factors play a role); consequently, optimism is not the only solution. But it is a major one.

Optimists are resilient. Their positive outlook on life protects their mentality in challenging circumstances. Dennis Charney, dean of research at the Mount Sinai School of Medicine, examined 750 Vietnam War veterans held as prisoners of war for six to eight years. They were tortured and kept in solitary confinement. But unlike many of their fellow veterans, they did not develop depression or post-traumatic stress disorder on release. After extensive interviews and tests, Charney found ten characteristics that set them apart. Optimism was on top, altruism second. A sense of humor and having something to live for (meaning in life) were important factors too.[10]

OPTIMISTS ARE MORE SUCCESSFUL

In 1983 a study of 104 life insurance agents showed the relationship between optimism and success. All 104 agents scored very high on the initial optimism test. After one year 59 of the 104 had quit.

The agents who scored in the less optimistic half were twice as likely to quit. Agents who scored in the least optimistic quarter were three times likelier to quit than the agents who scored in the most optimistic quarter.

And the top-half optimistic agents sold 20 percent more insurance than the less optimistic agents from the bottom half. The agents from the top quarter sold 50 percent more than the agents in the bottom quarter. This study showed that optimism predicted who survived and who sold the most.

Based on this study, insurance company MetLife decided to test all applicants for their optimism. The strategy made MetLife, which had lost the industry leadership to Prudential at that time, very successful, because employees who would have caused problems and would have quit earlier in the past were no longer hired to begin with. The choice for optimism helped MetLife regain industry leadership over Prudential.

In sports we see the same. Athletes that have an optimistic explanatory style are more successful. The thing that sets them apart is that they know how to come back from defeat. In his book *Learned Optimism*, Seligman tells the story about swimmer Matt Biondi, who won five gold medals at the 1988 Seoul Olympics.

A few months before the Olympics, Biondi and his teammates had participated in a test to determine their levels of optimism. He came out in the top quarter of an already highly optimistic team.

As part of the test Biondi's coach simulated defeat under controlled conditions in the pool. During his practice Biondi swam the hundred-meter butterfly all out. Biondi's time was 50.2 seconds—a very good time. However, his coach told him that his time had been 51.7 seconds—a bad time for Biondi. The coach told him to take a short rest and then swim the race again. This time Biondi clocked 50.0 seconds. Because of his optimistic explanatory time Biondi got faster—not slower—after defeat.

This test served him well. In his first two races in Seoul, Biondi disappointed. He took a bronze and a silver medal instead of the golds he had been expected to take. Had Biondi peaked too early? Was he not the superstar people had expected?

Although the press and the audience lost their faith in him, Biondi, confirming the test done by Seligman and his team months earlier, bounced back from defeat, and from his five remaining races he brought five gold medals back to the United States.

The research is clear: Optimism helps us cope with difficult life events. It supports resilience. It makes us happier and healthier. So it makes a lot of sense to learn how to become an (even better) optimist. That's what the next chapter is all about.

chapter 3

HOW TO BECOME AN (EVEN BETTER) OPTIMIST

Optimism can be learned. Even diehard pessimists can become more optimistic. Our brain is surprisingly flexible.

WHAT DO YOU SEE?

Now that you are aware of the happiness, health, and success that a lifestyle of optimism brings, you may wonder whether or not you are indeed an optimist.

Let's do a little test.

Have a look at this image.

What do you see?

Do you see a horseman coming to you?

Or do you see the horseman riding away from you?

You can see the horseman going in both directions. But what you see at first glance says a lot about your attitude.

If you saw the horseman coming to you, you tend to have a more optimistic mind-set.

If you saw the horseman riding away from you, you tend to be more of a pessimist.

TEST YOUR OPTIMISM

There is a more scientific way to test your optimism and pessimism levels. Scientists have been using "The Life Orientation Test" in many of the studies about the relationship between optimism and pessimism and (mental) health. The test incorporates ten statements. You need to indicate the extent of your agreement using the following scale:

0 = strongly disagree
1 = disagree
2 = neutral
3 = agree
4 = strongly agree

Be as honest as you can throughout and try not to let your response to one statement influence your response to other statements. There are no right or wrong answers. (You can also do this test at www.jurriaankamp.com/opti-test.)

___ 1. In uncertain times, I usually expect the best.
___ 2. It's easy for me to relax.
___ 3. If something can go wrong for me, it will.
___ 4. I'm always optimistic about my future.
___ 5. I enjoy my friends a lot.
___ 6. It's important for me to keep busy.
___ 7. I hardly ever expect things to go my way.
___ 8. I don't get upset too easily.
___ 9. I rarely count on good things happening to me.
___ 10. Overall, I expect more good things to happen to me than bad.

See page 81 for scoring.

THE DIFFERENCE BETWEEN OPTIMISTS AND PESSIMISTS

The good news is that even if you turn out to be more of a pessimist than you think or hoped to be, you can learn to become more optimistic. In fact, that can be surprisingly simple.

The key difference between optimists and pessimists is how they view success and failure. Pessimists see failure as permanent, personal, and pervasive, while optimists see it as temporary, nonpersonal, and specific. Their views on success are the opposite: Optimists see success as something long term and global, something that results from commitment and hard work. Pessimists, however, are more likely to view success as something short term, temporary, and accidental.

Imagine two students who receive the same poor grade on an exam. The first student thinks, "I'm such a failure. I always do poorly in this subject. I can't do it right." The other student thinks, "This test was very difficult. I will do better on my next test. It was my birthday yesterday, after all."

The two students exhibit different "explanatory styles." The first student sees a situation that happened because of her ("I'm bad at that subject") and that she cannot change. The second student sees the poor result as related to something outside her (the difficulty of the specific test) and feels confident that the negative event will not repeat itself. The first student is a pessimist. The second student is an optimist.

Another example: You are on a walk and you see your friend Sarah on the other side of the street. You wave, but Sarah doesn't wave back. In fact, she turns a corner without even noticing you. If you are a pessimist, your thoughts may go back to your last conversation with Sarah; you start thinking that you may have said something wrong and that Sarah is angry with you. Soon, troubling thoughts ruin your happy walk. The negative feelings of the pessimist lead to withdrawal and inaction. You don't bounce back from a setback. In fact you allow your negative feelings from one situation to pollute your next experience. Your life becomes miserable.

If you were an optimist, you would have had a very different response. You would have thought about all the possible causes for Sarah not seeing you. She could have forgotten to put in her contact lenses that morning; she may have been lost in thoughts of her own; or she simply may have had a bad day. As an optimist, you don't lose the connection with Sarah even if she doesn't wave back. You see the cause of the setback in your life as temporary, changeable, and local. You don't feel helpless. That's why optimists are happier and healthier people.

WE THINK OF OURSELVES AS OPTIMISTS OR PESSIMISTS

The crucial difference between optimists and pessimists lies in the things you tell yourself—your self-talk, that endless stream of unspoken thoughts that runs through your head every day. The non-waving Sarah is not present. It is you with your thoughts. And a lot of these thoughts came to you at a very early age. More often they are not even your own. We tell ourselves the wrong things because we have the voices of influential others—most often our parents—in our heads.

Take this example: As a small kid, you were playing with your younger brother and somehow play got out of hand and you hit him. Your angry mother responded, "That is mean. You are not going to have any friends at school if you behave that way."

With such a response, she was assigning you the character flaw of being mean, as something that is part of your personality. Something permanent, pervasive, and personal. Experiences like that may turn you into a pessimist. You begin to tell yourself that you are a mean person. The problem is that once established these negative pathways prepare you to respond pessimistically to most similar situations.

But if your mother had said, "I see you are having a hard time. Come here. I think you are hungry. Let's go a make a sandwich," such a response would have made the bad behavior temporary and specific to the situation and not connected to your personality. It would have paved the way for you to say you were sorry to your brother. Your sense of self would have been preserved and you could have remained the optimist you always were.

DON'T SAY ANYTHING TO YOURSELF THAT YOU WOULDN'T SAY TO ANYONE ELSE

Pessimists need to learn to change their self-talk to rediscover their optimism. If you want to become more optimistic, you need to identify the areas of your life that you tend to think negatively about. Most pessimists are not pessimistic about everything. Their pessimism flourishes in certain significant areas.

When you have identified the areas that are negative for you, check yourself regularly during the day. Are you finding your thoughts mainly negative? Then you need to learn to dispute your thoughts. You need to challenge your own thinking and try to look at possible alternative outcomes. You can learn to turn negative thinking into positive thinking. Here are some examples.

Negative Self-Talk	Positive Self-Talk
I've never done it before.	It's an opportunity to learn something new.
It's too complicated.	I'll tackle it from a different angle.
I don't have the resources.	Necessity is the mother of invention.
I'm not going to get any better at this.	I wasn't able to fit this into my schedule, but I can reexamine some priorities.
I'm too lazy to get this done.	I can try to make it work.
There's no way it will work.	Let's take a chance.

Negative Self-Talk	Positive Self-Talk
It's too radical a change.	I'll see if I can open the channels of communication.
No one bothers to communicate with me.	I'll give it another try.[1]

Pessimists need to practice positive self-talk and follow one simple rule: Don't say anything to yourself that you wouldn't say to anyone else. It is surprising how harsh and negative we can be toward ourselves while we remain nice to the people around us.

Various studies have confirmed that explanatory styles can be changed. Martin Seligman pioneered many of those studies. Seligman started the Penn Resiliency Program at the University of Pennsylvania for first-year college students, a notoriously vulnerable group. The program consists of twelve sessions in which students are taught how to change the types of thoughts that are consistent with the pessimistic explanatory style.

The program also teaches assertiveness, creative brainstorming, decision making, relaxation, and other coping skills. More than twenty studies over the past twelve years show that the Penn Resiliency Program reduces and prevents depression, decreases feelings of hopelessness, limits or prevents anxiety, and improves health.

The conclusion is clear: Optimism can be learned. But learned optimism is more than just positive thinking. It is not just about saying positive things to yourself when you are fine and things are going well. What you think when things are not going well—when you fail or when you experience setbacks—is crucial. That's where the power of optimism comes from. As Seligman writes in *Learned Optimism*: "Changing the destructive things you say to yourself when you experience the setbacks that life deals us is the central skill of optimism."

HOW POSITIVE ACTIONS CAN MAKE YOU AN OPTIMIST

Changing your self-talk works. But trying to think positively can be challenging. More recent research shows that changing your brain from pessimist to optimist can be even easier.

Imagine a toddler who is having a tantrum about something. Suddenly you point your finger toward the sky: "Do you see that bird?" Through her tears the girl looks up and gets distracted. Her eyes begin to follow the bird. Her mouth falls open, the crying stops, and in moments the tantrum is gone. You have succeeded in tricking the girl out of it. It's simple and very often successful.

You would think it's not so easy to trick an adult, but it actually is. Elaine Fox, director of the Affective Neuroscience Laboratory in the Department of Psychology at the University of Essex and author of *Rainy Brain, Sunny Brain: How to Retrain your Brain to Overcome Pessimism and Achieve a More Positive Outlook*, has done many scientific experiments that show that positive *actions* rewire your brain no matter what you think while doing these actions.

Fox: "A very common thing with depression or pessimism is that people really find it difficult to motivate themselves to do anything. But invariably if they do force themselves to do something, they generally do actually quite enjoy it. If you do that on a regular basis it becomes a kind of habit. It's about shifting the habits of the mind. It's really important to break up the normal way of doing things."

Doing something can be going to a movie you really wouldn't dream of seeing—it doesn't have to be a positive movie, just a *different* movie. Or you read a book or magazine that you normally wouldn't think about reading. Go to a restaurant that you never went to before. Take dance lessons. It can also be simply taking a different route to work. Fox: "The brain is very good at settling into a very habitual way of doing things. When we get used to something new, the brain doesn't really have to think about it anymore. It can just switch off and operate like 'oh yeah, we're doing this again.' It doesn't take much effort [to switch the brain]."

KEEP A DIARY, PLAY A GAME

Optimists tend to remember more of the nice things happening to them and they forget a lot more of the negative things. Their selective mind-set fuels their optimism. Pessimists do the complete opposite and remember all the negative things. One way to overcome the negative bias is to keep a diary for a few days and write down the things that happen to you. Simple things, like "I was frustrated because I missed the bus." And "I ran into my friend Peter in the store." You rate each of these incidents as either positive or negative. Then when they look back after a week or so, most people who are very pessimistic are surprised to find that they have forgotten that a lot of positive things that happen to them—more often far more than negative things. That awareness helps shifting the brain too. Research has shown that keeping such a diary helps to challenge and change the pessimistic pattern.

Scientists have developed a kind of "positive training" called "Cognitive Bias Modification" (CBM). The training consists of looking at a set of pictures of four people. One of them is smiling, the other three are looking angry. The challenge is to pick the smiling face the fastest. When you do this training a few minutes per day, research shows remarkable improvement after only hours of total practice. In one study, 72 percent of a group of people suffering from social anxiety disorder were cured after just two hours of practicing CBM. CBM can be done on an app (Anxiety Mint, Psych Me Up) or on the website http://baldwinlab.mcgill.ca/labmaterials/materials_BBC.html.

The best results with CBM are achieved when this training is combined with a mindfulness meditation for at least ten minutes per day, three days a week.

SMILE, HAVE FUN, TURN OFF THE TELEVISION, AND KEEP GOOD COMPANY

The simple act of smiling—using your "smile muscles"—can improve your mood. Having fun is also important, like listening to your favorite music or watching your favorite movie. When I have a bad day I love to watch a short YouTube video about how the Dutch soccer team beat Brazil at the 2010 World Championships. I have been doing this for a few years—granted, to the frustration of my family—not aware of the research that shows that such things really work.

It also helps to turn off the news and cancel the paper; as we have already seen, media feed pessimism. Interesting fact: When optimists and pessimists read the same newspaper, they are both drawn to the stories their minds seek. Pessimists see and remember the negative stories. Optimists tend to overlook those and their eyes go to the more positive news—which is a much harder job!

Keep good company is critical too. To move away from pessimism, it helps to surround yourself with optimists and not to join the ever-present complainers.

YOU NEED THREE FUN EXPERIENCES FOR EVERY BAD EXPERIENCE TO THRIVE

There's a good reason why our brain tends to drift to the negative. Thousands of years ago on the African plains, where the life of our ancestors started, a little sound in the bush could be a sign of imminent death. Fear made sense. Fear protected our ancestors. That's why our pessimism makes sense too.

However, there's less danger in the bush in our modern lives—in fact we have never had it so good (see chapter 4). But the good news that groundbreaking research by Barbara Fredrickson, professor of psychology at the University of North Carolina at Chapel Hill, has proven that we need to have three positive emotions for every negative one in order to thrive (some of the mathematical calculations used in Fredrickson's work have been discredited in further research. However, other psychologists, like Elaine Fox, support her general thesis of the importance of the 3 to 1 ratio).

Fredrickson's research shows that most people have about two positive experiences for every negative experience. These people do fine. However, your overall experience moves to flourishing and thriving when you are able to generate three positive experiences for every negative one.

We may pay more attention to negative events, but because we experience a greater frequency of positive events in our lives, most of us are not burdened by pessimism. But for true happiness—doing better than just fine—we need to aim higher and make sure that we have maintained the 3 to 1 ratio. As this chapter shows, that's much easier than it may seem. Positive events include listening to a piece of your favorite music; a moment of compassion or gratitude. A sense of wonder evoked by being in nature. Optimism stands always ready around the corner.

chapter 4

THE WORLD IS A BETTER PLACE
THAN YOU THINK

Turn off the television. Forget the news. The facts are
different than you are made to believe.

IT'S GETTING BETTER
ALL THE TIME

When you read the paper, surf the Web, or watch the news, you may conclude that our world is in dire straits. All indicators appear to point in the wrong direction. But that's not the case. It's the outcome of biased views based on the prevailing pessimism of our age. Compared to the recent and distant past we're doing much better on almost every front than our ancestors. And, yet, we keep hearing that the future will be nothing but disastrous. If 10,000 years and more is our guide, that's simply not true.

Here's an overview of the news you don't hear. It's our well-documented summary of the key indicators of the status of our lives and our societies. While in absolute terms there's still much progress to be desired, the overall trends are upward and positive. "I've got to admit it's getting better," the Beatles sang. Now it's your turn. Get ready for a true and happy experience: ten stories and statistics that show that the world is truly a better place than you think!

WE LIVE IN THE MOST
PEACEFUL ERA EVER

Let me begin with perhaps one of the biggest misconceptions. Despite what you hear on the news or read in the papers, and despite the stern and threatening announcements you hear at airports, the chances that you will be a victim of terrorism or violence are very, very small.

Just a few centuries ago, violence was pervasive. Beheadings were public entertainment. Heretics and witches were burned at the stake. Men beat their wives. Fathers beat their children. Slavery was common. There was continual war. For Steven Pinker, a prominent Harvard professor who has devoted more than ten years to studying the decline in violence, the conclusion is evident: We live in the most peaceful era ever.

That seems like a bold statement. After all, the twentieth century has a bad reputation. Millions died in two world wars, the Holocaust, the purges of Stalin and Mao. All this is true. It's very human to remember these terrible periods and forget that millions also died from violence in previous centuries. Pinker calls the decline in violence the most underappreciated trend in the history of the human species.

What drives that trend? Nation building curbed the drive to steal neighbors' land and the continual threat of hostile invasion. That allowed geopolitical stability to develop. The rise of democracy squelched the evils of tyrannical government. International trade turned countries into business partners, making peace economically attractive. Universal education provided an introduction to other cultures and views, opening old customs and practices to discussion.

And so began a genuine civilizing process in which the tempestuous rise of civilized behavior could be seen in everything from table manners to our approach to managing emotions. Where once a difference of opinion or an insult could easily lead to a knife fight with fatal consequences, with self-control people first counted to ten and swallowed their pride.

That trend continues unabated. In 1991, the FBI reported 758 cases of violent crime per 100,000 American residents; in 2010, the number was 404. The rate of murder and voluntary manslaughter halved in that same period. Worldwide data are fairly unreliable, of course, but here, too, the same development is visible. In 2002, ninety-four countries reported some 332,000 murders to the United Nations; in 2008, the number was 289,000. During that time, the number of reports declined in sixty-eight countries.

Today, you're more likely to drown in a swimming pool than die a violent death. That's a luxury no one outside this generation has ever known.[1]

OVERPOPULATION
IS A MYTH

We keep hearing it again and again: There's no way our world can become a healthier and better place because there are just too many of us. Overpopulation is seen as a major threat to the future of humanity.

Let's run the numbers for the 7 billion we are today. Let's assume that we all live in an average four-person family and we all have our own house with a small private garden on, say, a one-tenth of an acre lot. How much space do we need for that?

> 7,000,000,000 / 4 = 1,750,000,000 homes
> x 1/10 acre = 175,000,000 acres
> = 273,438 square miles

To put that in perspective: The state of Texas measures 268,820 square miles. So we can basically fit the whole current world population in just the second-largest state of the United States. Granted these people need food, water, freeways, and work, not just homes. But we can set up another state with offices. And we still have the rest of the United States for food farms. You get the idea . . . contrary to what you keep hearing, space is really not an issue on our planet.

And population growth?

That's not a problem either. Advanced countries like Italy and Japan face negative population growth. Their populations decline. That would also be the case in Germany were it not for net migration from other countries (which means that there are fewer people in these countries). The trend is the same around the globe: Where there's more wealth there are fewer births. Take India, the country that is predicted to overtake China as the country with the largest population. In 1950 Indian women had on average six children. Today that average is now 2.6—still a high number, but the trend is clearly downward and will continue in that direction with increasing wealth.

According to the most recent UN report on population, the world's population will stabilize during this century, or, at the latest, early next century, after which it will begin to decline. On average women across the globe give birth to 2.5 babies today—it was almost five in 1950. So the trend is downward. But even if the average woman has 0.5 more babies than the current rate in the next ninety years, the world population will peak at almost 16 billion in 2100. However, if the birth rate declines, with an average of 0.5 baby per woman, than we get to a world population of just over 6 billion in 2100. That's fewer people on the planet than we have today! With the current trend in world population growth leader India, that last outcome is not unimaginable at all.

So, worst case, we may need another Texas. But that's not the likeliest outcome. To put the numbers in yet another perspective: In 2011 the world celebrated the arrival of the 7 billionth person. If all of us would have come to the baby shower the state of Maryland would have offered plenty of space for everyone to dance.[2]

... AND WE CAN FEED
ALL THESE PEOPLE

Doomsayers keep referring to *Population Bomb* author Paul Ehrlich, who wrote in 1968: "The battle to feed all of humanity is over [that is, lost]. In the 1970s the world will undergo famines—hundreds of millions will starve to death."

That is true. We have seen very severe famines. And we keep witnessing these from time to time. That's very painful. But that doesn't mean that we are not able to grow enough food for the world population. Famine is more than anything a distribution problem. In India an estimated 40 percent of the harvest never reaches the market. In the United States about 40 percent of food is wasted, according to the Natural Resources Defense Council. Distribution is a challenge, but by no means an insurmountable one.

At the same time, the good news is that agricultural yields around the world have been steadily increasing. Consider a few figures. The area of the Earth's surface devoted to growing grain has hardly changed since 1965. Yields in tons, by contrast, have more than doubled. The production of a given quantity of crop requires 65 percent less land than it did in 1961, according to Jesse Ausubel and Iddo Wernick of Rockefeller University, and Paul Waggoner of the Connecticut Agricultural Experiment Station, in their 2013 paper "Peak Farmland and the Prospect for Land Sparing." The researchers find that over the next fifty years people are likely to release from farming a land area "1.5 times the size of Egypt, 2.5 times the size of France, or 10 Iowas, and possibly multiples of this amount." In other words: We are going to need less land to feed more people and we'll be able to preserve more wilderness.

A lot of this progress has to do with technology, but that doesn't mean we can only survive with genetically manipulated organisms (GMOs). To the contrary: ever more clever organic agriculture techniques—led by the University of California, Davis in the United States and Wageningen University in the Netherlands—and technology that allows for much more efficient use of water will make it possible to continue to harvest more food from the same amount of land in a healthy way for people and planet. Experiments around the world show that modern organic agriculture can deliver higher yields on farmland where topsoil has been damaged after years of heavy use of chemicals. More and more research confirms that organic agriculture can indeed feed the world.

And water? One more calculation. The Columbia River begins in the Canadian Rockies and ultimately dumps some 200 trillion liters of sweet water into the Pacific Ocean every year. That comes to almost 80 liters (about 20 gallons) per person—all 7 billion of us—per day. I'm not suggesting that getting enough drinking water to the world population is an easy job. But for a species that can send people in rockets to the moon surely this is not a challenge we cannot meet.[3]

WE ARE LIVING LONGER

We're living longer—and for those who savor life, with all its ups and downs, that's good news. A hundred years ago, our ancestors could expect fewer than fifty birthdays—and even that was nearly twenty more than the global average. In 2010, the worldwide average had risen to 67.2 years, and even 78.2 years in the United States. That increase is largely due to the progress of medical science. For example, better health care has dramatically reduced infant and maternal death rates. In poor countries, life expectancy is still rising sharply. In the past five decades, it has risen by ten years in Africa, despite wars and disease.

Not only has the immense grief of burying our children become a rarity; our grandparents are also living longer. The continuing increase in life expectancy in the West is largely the result of the over-eighty crowd living longer. In 1950, an eighty-year-old woman had only a 16 percent chance of making it to ninety; in 2002, that number was 37 percent.

The challenge now is to live our extra years in good health. The statistics on that haven't been around long enough to present a clear trend. But the available data from France,

Germany, Belgium, and other countries suggest that we not only live longer but also spend those extra years with milder complaints and fewer limitations on our daily lives.

Experts consider it unlikely that the upward trend in life expectancy will end any time soon. If the trend continues—and it has shown no sign of slowing since 1840—we can expect most babies born in rich countries after 2000 to live to be a hundred. A 2009 study in the *Lancet* concluded: "Continued progress in the longest-living populations suggests we are not close to a limit, and further rise in life expectancy is likely."[4]

DEMOCRACY IS SPREADING

For essentially all of human history, non-elected leaders—feudal lords—have governed groups of people almost everywhere in the world. Some leaders worked their way up through the ranks to become military or religious commanders; others enjoyed the happy accident of being the firstborn sons in royal families. The idea that all men and women may vote for a politician to represent them in their country's government is relatively new.

Forty years ago, American think tank Freedom House published its first annual report ranking the world based on democratic freedoms. A mere forty countries had free elections. Back then, Spain and Portugal were military dictatorships. Much has changed in the intervening decades. In the 1980s, many military regimes fell in Latin American countries, including Argentina and Brazil. In East and South Asia, too, modern civil freedoms arose. After communism fell apart, the 1990s brought democracy to Eastern Europe. Today, Freedom House counts eighty-seven nations as "free countries," a doubling in less than four decades. An additional sixty countries are "partly free," leaving forty-eight countries still labeled "not free."

The African continent and the Middle East are in a turbulent period of political change. In 1990, Freedom House counted just three African countries with multiparty systems, universal suffrage, regular fraud-free elections, and ballot secrecy. Today, with the exception of Mali, democracy is taking West Africa by storm. In violent hotbeds such as Sierra Leone and Liberia, political innovations have brought about great progress. Guinea and the Ivory Coast have ended periods of internal unrest and are once again democracies. US President Barack Obama has even praised Ghana's democracy. And the recent protests in countries such as Egypt, Syria, and Iran demonstrate people's willingness to fight to escape authoritarian regimes.

It's still unclear what kind of change the Arab Spring will bring. Democracy progresses in waves, not in a straight line. That's why a country like South Africa has plunged in every international ranking after the rise of democracy following the release of Nelson Mandela in the 1990s gave way again to a culture of nepotism and corruption. But the overall conclusion is clear. Despotic rulers are retreating and democracy is on the rise giving a voice to more and more people in more and more countries.[5]

WE HAVE MORE FREE TIME

Capitalism is a rat race, forcing us to work all the time, pushed by profit seeking and ruthless competition. We are busy, busy, busy. Right?

It looks quite different from an historical perspective. The amount of working hours per year for full-time employees has been on a steady decline for more than a century. In the late nineteenth century people worked an estimated ten hours per day for six days per week. Vacation didn't exist, nor retirement. People worked more than 3,000 hours per year.

The Organisation for Economic Co-operation and Development (OECD) average number for working hours for 2012 was 1,765 (US 1,790). That's 11 percent less than the average of 1,981 hours that OECD workers spent on the job in 1970.

The welfare state has gradually reduced the number of working hours. In the 1970s the five-day/forty-hour workweek became the norm. Today many European countries have a thirty-six-hour workweek.

Retirement has made a big difference as well. That was an "invention" by German Chancellor Otto von Bismarck. In 1889, when the Industrial Revolution was gathering steam, he decided that Germany would begin paying state pensions to people over the age of sixty-five. After a life of unremitting labor, people were often frail and sick, unfit for the back-breaking jobs that dominated that era and nearly ready for the casket. Indeed, Bismarck's creation of the first welfare state was mainly inspired by the fact that the elderly of the time were slowing productivity in the factories. Because few people lived beyond the age of seventy, it was not a great financial burden for the German state. If Bismarck were to make the same decision today, he would probably set the retirement age at eighty or even higher. In that sense the politicians who are trying to raise the retirement age at the moment have a point.

The biggest change in work experience, however, is just starting to get momentum. Since the days of Bismarck we have worked in big factories and big companies and institutions where we needed to report on time and where our productivity was monitored. That's why we have these nice statistics about the number of working hours. The Internet is radically changing that. The boundaries between "life" and "work" are getting blurred. On the negative side, that means responding to work emails during your private evening. But on the positive side, it means you can go surfing in the morning and then start your work in Starbucks whenever it suits you. At the same time fewer and fewer people will work in big organizations, and more and more will use the Web to be entrepreneurs with cheap access to a global market. We'll be creating our own jobs again, like we did before the Industrial Revolution. But we'll be able to do that in a much more efficient way than the carpenter or grocer of the past.

I know that many of us feel the burden of their work today. Stress is abundant. We need to learn to manage that. Yet, beyond the statistics, we have opportunities to make our own lives and work in ways no generation before us ever could. More and more we can make time, *our* time. That's even better than free time.[6]

WE ARE GETTING RICHER

These days, most poor families in the West have cell phones, televisions, washing machines, and cars. Their tap water is clean and their food safe to eat. Though I'm not trying to play down the problem of poverty, these conditions are a vast improvement over those in, say, the 1950s.

Until 1800, the value of the global economy hardly changed, though there were periods when things got somewhat better or worse. "The average person in the world of 1800 was no better off than the average person of 100,000 BC," Gregory Clark, professor of economics at University of California, Davis concludes in *Farewell to Alms: A Brief Economic History of the World.*

Journalist Matt Ridley has sought to show that people today are richer than Louis XIV was circa 1700, when he was the wealthiest man in the world's wealthiest country. He ate off gold plates, true, but his array of choices was startlingly paltry compared with the overwhelming selection in today's grocery stores. Louis might have had a tailor, a chauffeur, and

500 other servants, but today, all of us do, in the form of clothing stores and budget airlines.

Important things cost less today than ever before. That includes all the critical stuff: food, clothes, fuel, and shelter. Ridley calculates: In 1800, a candle providing one hour's light cost six hours' work. In the 1880s, the same light from a kerosene lamp took fifteen minutes' work to pay for. In 1950, it was eight seconds. Today, it's half a second. In these terms, we are 43,200 times better off than we were in 1800.

The Industrial Revolution changed everything. People left for the cities, general health improved, schools were built. For the past two centuries, the economy has grown spectacularly, and everyone has profited.

Yes, but inequality . . . ?

Three billion people still live on less than $2.50 per day. And the eighty-five wealthiest people together own as much as all these 3 billion together.

Yes, that's true.

It's also true that the proportion of Vietnamese living on less than $2 per day has dropped from 90 percent to 30 percent in the past two decades.

Another example: Ghana's gross domestic product (GDP) per capita today stands at the same level as that of Spain in 1950 (in the same 1990 dollars). We would not argue that Spain in 1950 was a poor and hopeless place.

The gap is closing. According to the most pessimistic long-term UN estimates, the economies of rich countries will continue to grow at an average of 1 percent per year and the developing world at an average rate of 2.3 percent. That means that by the end of this century, our great-grandchildren in rich nations will be two and a half times wealthier than we are, and people in poor countries will be at least nine times wealthier than their ancestors living today.

The gap is also closing because many of the poorest are also the youngest people in low-paid jobs at the beginning of their careers, whereas many of the wealthiest are older people whose income is not going to rise much more. Statistics show that 80 percent of the people born in households below the poverty line will escape poverty when they reach adulthood. We're definitely not there yet, but we are certainly on a good track.[7]

NATURAL RESOURCES ABOUND

Another favorite part of the pessimists' mantra is that there will be too many people and not enough food, water, and natural resources (energy).

Let me begin with oil.

In 1970, there were 550 billion barrels of proven oil reserves in the world. In the following twenty years the world consumed 600 billion barrels. So we should have been at minus 50 billion barrels in 1990. However, proven reserves totaled 900 billion barrels that year. Today that total stands at more than 1,400 billion barrels. Yes, there's an end to oil, but we are not going to reach that any time soon, and new technologies and discoveries are emerging every day. More important, there are much better and cleaner alternatives that are rapidly becoming competitive.

At the time of the 1973 oil crisis, the then-Saudi Arabian oil minister Sheikh Zaki Yamani spoke wise words: "The Stone Age did not end for lack of stone, and the Oil Age will end long before the world runs out of oil."

It's the same with other raw materials. Figures from industry show that reserves are growing. Limestone, aluminum, iron, copper, gold, nitrogen, and zinc—the nonfuels—account for more than 75 percent of the worldwide expenditure on hard commodities, and despite a spectacular increase in our

consumption of all these substances—by a factor of 2 to 10—
the available reserves of every one of them *grew* in the second
half of the past century. That's because we recycle intelligently,
and we've consistently searched for more.

Increasing consumption also means that prices fall over
the long term. They've long *been* falling, fluctuations not-
withstanding: Since 1845, the price index for industrial commodities—neatly tracked and corrected for inflation by the
Economist—has fallen by an average of 70 percent. Ever more
and ever cheaper: *What* commodities crisis?

Finally, please note that we aren't interested in these resources as such. We need them for the services they can provide. Two thousand years ago nobody could imagine uranium
as a source for energy. We are going to find new ways to com-
bine, use, and reuse all those atoms to enable us to do the
things we want. At some point in the future people will look
back at us like we look back at the ancient Romans—clever people, leaders in their times, but, boy, what a primitive society.[8]

OUR FOOD IS SAFER

For centuries, people prayed before meals—but, especially,
they prayed *for* them. For practically all of human history, life
has consisted of a struggle for food—and in too many parts of
the world, it still is. Today, those of us in rich countries appear
to have forgotten that not so long ago, gathering, cleaning,
and preparing food took up a substantial part of every day.
Not only was it time-consuming work, there was always a
chance bacteria would make you sick.

Today, every news report on horsemeat or dioxin in
chickens causes a shock wave. We easily forget that our food
is safer than it's ever been. Only rarely does what we eat make
us sick. It's pretty hard these days to contract old-fashioned
food poisoning. We owe this development to scientific progress, ingenious quality controls at every stage of production,

and improved storage methods. In the early twentieth century a simple glass of milk was a primary source of tuberculosis. With pasteurization, the danger of milk was suddenly gone.

In recent decades, great strides have been made against microbial and chemical contamination. You can go into a restaurant knowing that the chances that you'll get sick are miniscule. In the United States, one person in 100,000 dies of a foodborne illness every year. These cases often result from negligence in the system—something we can reduce by sharpening legislation, standards, and inspection.

Nowadays the bigger risks in food are of a completely different kind. The danger is not in the potential presence of bacteria; it lies with the ingredients that are used by profit-driven food multinationals. They use, for instance, a suspicious sweetener, high-fructose corn syrup, that's linked to type 2 diabetes. In other words: Food may still not be completely safe. Yet the fact that you can eat almost anywhere without getting sick is a huge achievement that the modern citizen hardly appreciates.[9]

RACISM IS ON THE DECLINE

We tend to look at absolute facts. And that's good. It keeps motivating us to change things for the better. Many of the trends mentioned in this chapter require more effort, much more effort. That certainly applies to racism. The United States may have its first black president, but racism still exists. He knows that. We all do. Offensive ethnic chants are routinely banned from sports stadiums, and children are still punished for skin-color taunts.

At the same time, a lot of progress has been made and is being made. The time when racism in America was a destabilizing social problem that led to structural violence and injustice really does seem to be over.

The success of the civil rights movement doesn't mean there are no problems today. In America, nearly 40 percent of the prison population is black, such a high percentage that socioeconomic differences hardly provide an adequate explanation. Unemployment among Native Americans is higher than for any other ethnic group—up to 69 percent in reservation populations. Moreover, racial strife still sometimes causes death and destruction in plenty of places—consider Sudan and Rwanda. But even in Europe, periodic waves of violence break against the Romani or immigrants from the Middle East.

Yet a lot of progress is being made too. One of the most inspiring experiences is walking in busy city centers of Brazilian cities like São Paulo and Rio de Janeiro and watching teenagers of all colors and races leave their high schools hand in hand. That new Brazilian generation has left the issue behind and stands as an example for the rest of the world, where travel and trade keep mixing people more and more together.

The best evidence for the decline in racism is the rise of interracial marriages. Every day people of different races interact, fall in love, and have children together. Each new generation is more ethnically and culturally diverse than ever before.

In 1970, interracial marriages constituted just 2 percent of all American marriages; 2010 US Census reports 10 percent and a 28 percent increase compared to 2000. California, which so often shows the way to the future, already has almost 13 percent interracial marriages. The European Union lags behind, with interracial marriages at just about 5 percent. However, in Europe as well the numbers are rising year after year. That shows that racism is slowly but surely retreating.[10]

chapter 5

WELCOME TO THE AGE OF OPTIMISM

We offer a preview of what the future may bring as innovation and creativity continue to flow.

THE BEST IS YET TO COME

Optimism is a journey, not a destination.

The evolution continues. We keep facing new challenges. But new opportunities arise every day as well. Yesterday's solutions turn into today's problems. But the best news is that new ideas and new stories keep emerging faster and faster, driving a new age of optimism that will overcome the prevailing—but unnecessary—forces of pessimism and providing the greatest opportunities for you and your fellow optimists to lead a more fulfilling life. The last thing you want is a perfect world because that's a world that doesn't need you. Stay tuned for some perspectives that should be part of every optimist's toolkit and for a discovery—sometimes merely anecdotal—of some domains that will determine the future, *your* future. The best is yet to come!

PREDICTING THE FUTURE IS HARD, BUT IT'S IMPOSSIBLE IF YOU'RE TOO PESSIMISTIC

Humankind continuously exceeds its own expectations in the development of new technology. However, we are really bad at one thing: predicting that development. And that's a problem that leads to a lot of unnecessary pessimism.

The following quotes should silence the widespread pessimism about the future:

> Our numbers are burdensome to the world, which can hardly support us.
>
> —Tertullian, Christian author who lived in the second century CE

> The abdomen, the chest and the brain will forever be shut from the intrusion of the wise and humane surgeon.
>
> —Sir John Eric Ericson, surgeon to Queen Victoria, 1873

Heavier-than-air flying machines are impossible.

—Lord Kelvin, mathematician and physicist, 1895

It is an idle dream to imagine that automobiles will take the place of railways in the long distance movement of passengers.

—American Railroad Congress, 1913

Who the hell wants to hear actors talk?

—H. M. Warner, cofounder of Warner Brothers, 1927

There is no hope for the fanciful idea of reaching the Moon because of insurmountable barriers to escaping the Earth's gravity.

—Forest Ray Moulton, astronomer, 1932

There is not the slightest indication that [nuclear energy] will ever be obtainable. It would mean that the atom would have to be shattered at will.

—Albert Einstein, 1932

Television won't be able to hold on to any market it captures after the first six months. People will soon get tired of staring at a plywood box every night.

—Darryl F. Zanuck, head of 20th Century-Fox, 1946

The world potential market for copying machines is 5,000 at most.

—IBM to the eventual founders of Xerox, 1959

There is no reason for any individual to have a computer in their home."

—Ken Olson, president of Digital Corporation, 1977

THE AGE OF OPTIMISM 1:
GROWTH AND ENERGY FOR ALL

The morning shower, usually at half past six, is one of my favorite moments of the day. Yet the shower is also a wonderful example of the excesses of the modern Western lifestyle. Despite water-saving showerheads, every day we rinse millions of gallons of clean water into the sewers while at the same time thousands of people are dying because they don't have safe drinking water. No, my daily shower is at first sight not a positive contribution to a better, more sustainable world.

However, during my morning shower I undoubtedly enjoy my most creative moments of the day. With the falling water comes a flow of new ideas and insights. Most of my new plans are born in the shower. And I think that my contribution to a better world would have been far less if I had spent less time under the shower. I would have wasted less water, yet I also would have come to less positive contributions. To continue my contribution to a better world, I better keep showering.

The usual discussion about sustainability is like my shower dilemma. Too often we confuse sustainable growth with less growth. The focus is on doing as much as possible with less. We are supposed to stay put because the supply of natural resources is finite or because there are already too many people on the planet.

It is a misconception that economic growth and sustainability are mutually exclusive. Nature is characterized by continuous abundant growth; by continuous problem solving. There is no way I can tell the orange tree in our garden to take it a little easy next season. But that is nonetheless the message citizens and businesses continuously get: You need to reduce your CO_2 emissions and your ecological footprint. Those are fine objectives, but we must reach them through innovation and progress and with the enthusiasm with which we have embraced the Internet and mobile phones—not through a defensive retreat.

Don't get me wrong. This is not a plea to maximize oil consumption. The question is, *how* do we grow our economies? We can use a lot more clean energy than we do, and governments have the tools to promote that. Germany is the country with the highest percentage of solar panels in the world. And that's not because that Northern European country captures the most sunshine. It is very simple: If we put limits on growth—if only in our sustainability policy views and considerations—we will have fewer solar panels and fewer other climate solutions.

The transformation of energy and related distribution systems provide tremendous opportunities for continued economic growth toward a cleaner and more prosperous world, while at the same time providing increasing opportunities for more and more people.

Somewhere in the not-too-distant future, a new kind of Google will emerge, an energy company or energy system that will change the world even more radically than the Internet has done so far.

Although the Internet is growing explosively, there are still billions of people who are not part of the digital revolution. But even the poorest inhabitants of the planet need energy every day. It is hard to imagine how big the market for clean energy is and how much the pioneers of this surging energy revolution will be rewarded. Every optimist should take a shower and jump on the opportunities.

THE AGE OF OPTIMISM 2: SUSTAINABLE ABUNDANCE

Nature is a superb problem solver. The R&D department of nature has been around for millions of years and handsomely beats recently invented machines.

Humanity has always looked at nature. We saw birds; we made aircrafts. But compared to nature, our machines are clunky, and they leave a lot of waste. Nature is both very efficient and abundant. Nature produces cheaply, cleanly and leaves no waste. Sustainability, in a dynamic sense, is not a target for nature; it is a given. If you add the mass of all ants on the planet together, they apparently weigh more than the 7 billion of us do—no idea how that calculation was done. The ants travel, work, and build, but they leave no trace of waste.

The good news is that today's technology now allows us to both observe—through video technology—and imitate—through nanotechnology—nature better than ever before. Icarus and Daedalus could not have dreamed of the work David Lentink, assistant professor mechanical engineering, is doing these days in his lab at Stanford University.[1]

Lentink invited students around the world to work with him and take videos of birds and insects. He sent the students the fastest digital cameras available (3,300 frames per second). With these cameras you can see things that the human eye can't see.

In his lab Lentink studies the videos in slow motion and sees things no one has ever seen. One example: We have all witnessed flocks of ducks rising from a lake and starting to fly in a perfect V-formation. Lentink received lots of videos of that same phenomenon. In slow motion he saw in all these videos that just as the ducks rise from the water and build their formation, some of them start flying on their backs. They turn around and continue in the formation upside down.

So far Lentink has no idea why the ducks do this. But he knows for sure that nature has a reason, and he is determined to find out. Ultimately, work like his will contribute to better planes. Lentink's example is just one of many through which lessons from nature are learned to solve human problems. There are flame retardants made from citrus rather than from hazardous chemicals; there are paints that repel water like the skin of an animal; razorblades from renewable silk and paints that capture solar energy. The list gets longer every day. Technology is driving a new Industrial Revolution that's going to drive and inspire optimists for years to come: The Natural Revolution.

THE AGE OF OPTIMISM 3:
MONEY THAT SERVES PEOPLE AND SOCIETY

When systems don't work, they open the playing field for improvements. The current financial system serves that famous 1 percent and has caused and is still causing tremendous suffering to billions of people. Just that fact alone provides an enormous market opportunity. The first experiments with Internet currencies are already happening.

The current money system is driven by interest and therefore by scarcity. When banks create money—through the distribution of loans—only the principal amount of the loan is created, the interest is not created. But the interest still has to be paid, so there's a continuous competition for money. We don't know more than that there's always a shortage of money. There is not enough money for schools, for pensions, for hospitals, for art, for environmental protection, for playgrounds. There's not enough money in most of our private lives. We talk about unemployment, but it is not that there are no jobs. There's no money to pay for these jobs, for the work that needs to be done.

Moreover, the current financial system is very volatile and unpredictable because each country has a currency monopoly. As is clear from the sciences of biology and physics, healthy ecosystems consist of a diverse range of interacting players. The interactivity provides balance and feedback and makes systems resilient, stable, and robust. Monopolies don't work in the economy either. That's why governments legislate against and break up business monopolies. The currency system is still an exception, but given its incredible negative impact it's hard to imagine that it will stay that way.

The key function of money is to facilitate exchanges and trade. Experiments with interest-free complementary currencies have shown that it is possible to enable transactions that would otherwise not have happened. Complementary currencies can make money available when it is needed and can pay for work that needs to be done.

You may be familiar with some local complementary currency systems, and you may think that these seem to offer a well-meant but not very practical return to the days of barter. However, interest-free complementary money systems can be very modern, and you are likely to be part of those without even realizing it.

Frequent-flyer programs are successful complementary money systems. You can buy lots of things with air miles—not just tickets. Air miles have a value; they are money. There are more than 15 trillion air miles in circulation; that is more than dollar bills. Or think about the bonus card you use at your supermarket.

Internet currencies like Bitcoins are not interest free. But the technology, once tested, can be used in different ways. Many solutions will flow from breaking up the current national money monopolies and the introduction of interest-free complementary currencies.

THE AGE OF OPTIMISM 4: MEDITATION FOR PEACE

Meditation and yoga have been released from their Asian boundaries and travel the world. More and more research confirms the health and happiness benefits for those who practice regularly. But this swelling spiritual wave drives a trend that has an even bigger potential. As research has shown, groups of meditators can calm down societies and reduce violence.

Once, long ago, rulers in India kept monks close to their courts. They knew the ascetics' daily meditations had a calming effect on the populace. The kings took care of the monks so they could care for society.

Research shows that as one meditator settles at a higher level of consciousness it leads to more coherent brain patterns; her contribution to the overall energy field is such that it lifts everybody else. Psychologist Fred Travis has shown that someone meditating alone in a room has a positive effect on another person doing a cognition test in an adjacent room. The increased coherence of the meditator "spilled over" to the nonmeditator, who was not aware of the meditator in the other room. The conclusion: When the brain coherence of the nonmeditator was better, she did better on the test.[2]

The coherence-building effect becomes even stronger when meditation is practiced in groups and brainwaves synchronize. Roger Nelson, who leads the Global Consciousness Project at Princeton University, has measured the impact of 2,500 advanced Transcendental Meditation meditators in Fairfield, Iowa, during a fourteen-week summer program. The group meditated for an hour both morning and evening, and he correlated these times with the activity of machines that generate random numbers, which the Global Consciousness Project has installed worldwide. Nelson is unequivocal in his conclusion. "When human consciousness becomes coherent and synchronized," he says, "the behavior of random systems changes."[3]

Perhaps the most mind-blowing study was done in 1993. At the time, the District of Columbia was seen as "the murder capital of the world." During the summer a group of more than 2,500 meditators got together. The Metropolitan Police Department of the District of Columbia, the FBI, twenty-four independent criminologists, and social scientists from major institutions like the University of Maryland and the University of Texas collaborated on the study. Meditation sessions were held in locations around the city. The study showed a 23 percent reduction in homicide, rape, and assault.[4]

Ancient wisdom is being rediscovered. The impact of this research opens a whole new perspective on the organization of society. Meditation has the potential to reduce violence and conflict in the world—and at a fraction of annual military spending.

THE AGE OF OPTIMISM 5: MIND OVER MATTER

In modern Western medicine, disease is something that needs to be eradicated with pharmaceutical drugs or surgery. But what if each disease has a message, perhaps a critical message that provides an opportunity for the healing of the soul? It's a perspective that would turn modern medicine upside down.

German physician Rüdiger Dahlke wrote the book *The Power of Illness*. He argues that we create disease with our psyches, with our mental behavior, and that's also the fundamental level where healing begins. Disease, then, is not something we should try to avoid; it is our opportunity to become more aware and to find out why we are alive. We learn our life's lessons and purpose through our illnesses and ailments.

The idea that our physiology and psychology can have an effect on one another has been around in the Western world for some 1,000 years, and the two were always integrated in the ancient Asian traditions. It caught the interest of Sigmund Freud in the beginning of the twentieth century, but Dahlke goes further and says that all disease has a psychological meaning. That disease offers the chance to heal our souls.

He was doing psychotherapy sessions with his patients when he found out that body and soul operate on very parallel tracks. Patients who were constipated had a hard time opening up in the psychotherapy sessions. Subsequently, after these patients had started fasting—which resolved their constipation—the psychotherapy became much more effective. Dahlke: "The disease is the symbol of a task. If we perform the task, we relieve the body. If you don't get the message on the psychological level, the challenge manifests in the body and you have to live the illness."

Living disease, rather than fighting it, has led to many examples of "miraculous" recoveries under Dahlke's guidance in Europe. He saw people being cured from cancer, diabetes, multiple sclerosis, rheumatism, and more. As important, his work—and that of others—points medicine in a new and very different, less invasive, and less expensive direction. The reinvention of medicine is a key project of the age of optimism.

THE AGE OF OPTIMISM 6:
FOOD IS THE BEST MEDICINE

I once tried to drive my regular gas car after filling the tank with diesel. I didn't get very far. The experience taught me an important lesson in a painful way. It makes a difference how you feed an engine. Our bodies are engines too. In fact, they are among the most complex and efficient energy systems on our planet. So, one would assume that we would pay attention to the "gas" we put in our delicate systems.

However, apart from obvious exceptions such as sports, the relationship between food and performance of the human body is still a largely unexplored area. Just visit a regular supermarket or even a mainstream hospital. If the relationship between food and health would be widely accepted, the food offered in these places would look very, very different.

Yet, for good health, plain foods without any additions are the best. As research shows, it's hard to beat the simple apple as the most healthy food item.

But the tide is changing. Mainstream doctors are writing bestsellers about how we can prevent or heal disease with food. Just two examples: Mark Hyman, M.D., who helped President Bill Clinton recover from heart disease, prescribes how to lose weight, overcome diabetes, and prevent disease in *The Blood Sugar Solution*. And David Perlmutter, M.D., explains in *The Grain Brain*, based on extensive research, how the sugar and grains in our diet provoke the inflammation that is behind most degenerative illnesses, and that even dementia can be reversed through the proper diet.

We would live in a different, far more healthy and peaceful world—where the forces of optimism would be much stronger instantly—if all of us would just eat the produce that the soil of the Earth abundantly provides.

THE AGE OF OPTIMISM 7:
WE CREATE OUR OWN REALITY

Mainstream medicine rules that the genes that we receive at birth determine our health. That means we don't create our own lives. We are victims of our genes. That's a rather depressing perspective that aligns with the strong forces of pessimism in society. But is it true?

Recent research points in another direction. Stem cell biologist Bruce Lipton took genetically identical stem cells and put them in separate Petri dishes and then changed the environment in those dishes. In one dish the cells formed muscle tissue, in the second dish they formed bone tissue, and in the third dish they formed fat cells. Identical cells developed in three different directions through changing of the environment. Different information from the environment led genes to evolve in different ways. So genes are not pre-programmed to deliver certain results; they respond to information.

Lipton's discoveries are part of an emerging new biological paradigm that presents a radically different view on the evolution of life: epigenetics. *Epi* means "above" in Greek. *Epigenetics* means control *above* the genes. Lipton: "It turns out that as we move from one environment to another environment, we change our genetic read-out. Or, if we perceive that our environment is not supporting us, than that perception also changes our genetics."

The impact on medicine is profound. "Our health is really based on our perception and our beliefs and attitudes. If we find ourselves in a negative environment, or we perceive ourselves to be in a negative environment, we generally contribute to disease. If you want to recover health, you don't need to add medicine, you actually have to return yourself to a supportive, healthy environment and/or a healthy belief and the cells will heal themselves," says Lipton.[5]

Medical science is confirming Lipton's view. Studies show that sick people who are supported with some kind of mental training heal faster and better. Research also shows that 90 percent of the cases of cancer and heart disease—the two biggest killers on the planet—have nothing to do with genes but everything to do with lifestyle. In other words: We may need a coach as much as a doctor when we are ill. The optimistic perspective is that we can influence our health and we can heal ourselves.

THE AGE OF OPTIMISM 8:
WE CAN CHANGE OUR PERSONALITIES

Remember what you promised yourself on New Year's Day? Most New Year's resolutions disappear from our daily routines in weeks, if not days. Why is that? The explanation is that we are hard-wired against change. And there are good and useful reasons for that.

As a child we learn how life works. We learn to talk and walk. We learn that we cannot put our hands in fire. We store all that acquired knowledge somewhere in our memory that's operated by our brain. Our brain automates these procedures like a computer and stores the information in our subconscious. Just imagine that you would need to consciously think about how to walk each time you want to move. Without brain automation and our subconscious, our lives would be impossible.

Here's the problem: We don't only store the useful stuff like how to walk or talk. We also store and automate many unhelpful conclusions. As a five-year-old you may have had some unpleasant experiences in your home. There may have been stress because your mother or father lost a job. Because of the stress you received less attention—love—from your parents, and somehow you concluded that there was something wrong with you. You started feeling insecure, unloved, unworthy. . . . Wrong conclusion. Nonetheless, in our clever system, such a response gets automated too, and a sense of unworthiness gets hard-wired.

Many of us have seen therapists and have discovered such patterns. Yet it is very hard to change something that is, after all, part of your subconscious. Even if you consciously recognize a pattern, how do you change the subconscious "code"?

Neuroscience is one of the most exciting fields of science at the moment. The brain and consciousness are no longer inaccessible domains, and scientists are finding that the way the brain processes information can be manipulated to reduce stress, help repair damaged brains, enhance creativity, and improve (mental) health.

Neurotherapy reads brain waves, feeds them into a computer, and translates them into visual, audible, or tactile form.

The goal: By seeing, hearing, or touching your brain waves, you can (re)train your brain to produce desired levels of activity, and you can clean up overstressed parts of your brain or self-sabotaging brain processes.

Just imagine regular neurofeedback sessions at schools where children can learn to reset early childhood traumas and change their damaged personalities. Fewer troubled kids will lead to more healthy adults and less violence. And more optimism.

WHY EVERY DROP IN THE OCEAN MATTERS

The perspectives about the future I describe in this chapter are just a few in our ever-evolving world. There's a universe full of possibility open to you. There are endless more challenges to be met and solutions to be discovered. I'm sure there is an almost perfect correlation between the needs that are to be fulfilled and the talents that each of us brings to this world. Yet many of us hold back for fear of failure. We continue in our jobs, fulfilling someone else's mission rather than our own, preferring security above our shot at fulfillment and success. We tell ourselves that it doesn't matter; that our contribution will be small anyway; that whatever we can do won't be more than just a drop in the ocean.

Rosamund and Benjamin Zander recount a story originally from an essay by Loren Eisely in their book *The Art of Possibility*: Strolling along the edge of the sea, a man catches sight of a young woman who appears to be engaged in a ritual dance. She stoops down, then straightens to her full height, casting her arm out in an arc. Drawing closer, he sees that the beach around her is littered with starfish, and she is throwing them one by one into the sea. He lightly mocks her: "There are stranded starfish as far as the eye can see, for miles up the beach. What difference can saving a few of them possibly make?" Smiling, she bends down and once more tosses a starfish out over the water, saying serenely, "It certainly makes a difference to this one."

THE REAL ROSA PARKS STORY
IS YOUR STORY

We all know the story of Rosa Parks. We know how she fueled the civil rights movement by refusing to give up her place on the bus. Hers is the story of a rare hero who became "the mother of the civil rights movement." Or so we think. In his book *Soul of a Citizen*, Paul Rogat Loeb tells Parks's real story, and that reality is even more inspiring.

Rosa Parks was not just a bus passenger. When she boarded that bus in Montgomery, Alabama, she had been an active member of the National Association for the Advancement of Colored People (NAACP) for twelve years. The summer before, Parks had attended a ten-day training session at Tennessee's labor and civil rights organizing school, the Highlander Center, where she had met an older generation of civil rights activists.

In other words: Parks's decision to stay in her seat on the bus didn't come out of nowhere. That decision was a logical next step in her biography. That does not in any way detract from its historical importance and her tremendous courage, but it reminds us that this influential act might have never happened without the humble, frustrating work that preceded it. The real story of Rosa Parks tells us that every drop in the ocean counts.

It is not fate that someone becomes a hero and someone else not. Heroes, like Rosa Parks, went step by step along the path of their own beliefs, developing their unique talents, their truth. The strength to carry out their "heroism" is built up through hard work. The eighteenth-century Rabbi Zusya said, "God will not ask me: 'Why were you not Moses?' He will ask me: 'Why were you not Zusya?'" Or as we can say now: God will not ask you why you were not Rosa Parks. God will ask you, "Why were you not you?"

THERE ARE JUST NOT ENOUGH PROBLEMS FOR THE SOLUTIONS THAT WE HAVE

We live in a time of unprecedented opportunity. No generation before us has had such an access to ideas and growth. Why?

Sharing, exchanging has always been the driver of progress. In 1776 Adam Smith identified in *An Inquiry into the Nature and Causes of the Wealth of Nations* one primary cause for progress: "The propensity to truck, barter and exchange one thing for another." Almost 250 years later, trade is a multitude of times easier than it was in the days of the Scottish philosopher.

Borders have mostly disappeared—at least for goods and services. One in three citizens of the world already has access to the Internet. That means that they have instant access to all new ideas and innovations as they emerge. And what that means is well described by Matt Ridley in *The Rational Optimist*: "Exchange is to cultural evolution as sex is to biological evolution." We know what happens when people have sex. We are now witnessing what happens—in Ridley's words—"when ideas have sex."

It leads to an ongoing and ever-increasing explosion of new ideas, inventions, discoveries, and innovations. When the telephone had sex with the computer, the Internet was born. The old world of industrial production often has to deal with diminishing returns. At some point it becomes too expensive to dig for a certain raw material, for instance. But the world of ideas has a never-ending positive feedback loop. Solutions keep coming.

This is a book about the power of optimism, but we don't want to ignore the challenges that our world faces. To the contrary, we want to use optimism to address those challenges.

Yes, the whole world is getting better and richer at the moment, and there are things we can do to make the 3 billion people living on $2.50 a day benefit even faster.

We can get rid of out-of-date polluting processes and swiftly implement clean energy and reverse global warming.

We can create much better support systems for our health.

For each of these challenges there are many answers. But the world needs more optimists to discover those more quickly. The world needs more people like you to step up and take your place as contributor, problem solver, or inventor. We all possess the unique talents that we need to provide unique answers.

For 200 years, pessimists—from the Luddites who fought against the Industrial Revolution to the manure-worriers a century ago who saw more and more horses pollute the cities and couldn't imagine the solution the automobile was about to bring and today's climate change defeatists—have received most of the attention (and bestsellers and Nobel Peace Prizes) despite the fact that optimists have far more often been right.

We need to realize what a gift we give ourselves and the environment and the community around us when we let go of the pessimism bias and embrace our inherent problem-solving, optimistic natures. There are 7 billion of us. Each with her or his contributions and solutions and all of us increasingly connected. We can fail only because we don't act and we don't open ourselves for the world of possibility around us. If we act, we will soon discover that there are just not enough problems for the solutions that we have.

CHECKLIST FOR OPTIMISTS

____ No matter what happens, you're not a victim. It's up to you to determine your response.

____ Embrace your life's purpose. Make your own unique contribution that turns your environment into a better place and fulfills you.

____ Make *the* reality *your* reality.

____ Don't be distracted by the overwhelmingly negative news around you. Instead, read *The Intelligent Optimist*!

____ Don't look back too often. Keep yourself open to today's new opportunities.

____ Keep good company. Listen to your friends and loved ones, but don't become dependent on what others think of you.

____ Be grateful for everything life has given you and for every step forward you can take.

____ Make sure you laugh often. Don't take yourself too seriously.

SCORING LIFE ORIENTATION TEST

1. Reverse code items 3, 7 and 9 prior to scoring (0=4) (1=3) (2=2) (3=1) (4=0)

2. Add items 1, 3, 4, 7, 9, and 10 to obtain overall score.

   Total = 19–24   *High optimism*
   Total = 14–18   *Moderate optimism*
   Total =   0–13   *Low optimism*

Note: Statements 2, 5, 6, and 8 are filler items only. They are not scored.

Reference: Scheier, M.F., Carver, C.S., and Bridges, M.W. Distinguishing Optimism from Neuroticism (and Trait Anxiety, Self-Mastery and Self-Esteem): A Re-Evaluation of the Life Orientation Test. *Journal of Personality and Social Psychology* 67, 1994, 1063–78.

NOTES

Introduction: Stories, News, and the Challenge of Optimism

1. John Tierney, Good News Beats Bad on Social Networks, March 18, 2013.

2. Rolf Dobelli, "News Is Bad for You—and Giving Up Reading It Will Make You Happier, *Guardian*, April 12, 2013.

3. Ibid.

4. Attila Szabo and Katey L. Hopkinson, Negative Psychological Effects of Watching the News in the Television: Relaxation or Another Intervention May Be Needed to Buffer Them!, *International Journal of Behavioral Medicine* 14, June 2007, 57–62.

Chapter 1: The Best Way to Live

1. Interview with Geoff Ward to celebrate the fifth anniversary of Wilson's first book, *The Outsider*. http://www.colinwilsonworld.co.uk/.

2. Benjamin Zander, interview with the author, *Intelligent Optimist*, May/June 2013.

Chapter 2: A Key to Health, Happiness, and Success

1. M. A. Visintainer, J. R. Volpicelli, and M. E. P. Seligman, Tumor Rejection in Rats after Inescapable or Escapable Shock, *Science* 216, 1982, 437–39.

2. G. M. Buchanan and M. E. P. Seligman, Explanatory Style and Heart Disease, in *Explanatory Style* 1995, 225–32.

3. E. Giltay, J. Geleijnse, F. Zitman, T. Hoekstra, and E. Schouten, Dispositional Optimism and All-Cause and Cardiovascular Mortality in a Prospective Cohort of Elderly Dutch Men and Women. *Archives of General Psychiatry* 61, 2004, 1126–45.

4. H. Rasmussen, M. Scheier, and J. Greenhouse, Optimism and Physical Health: A Meta Analytic Review. *Annals of Behavioral Medicine* 37, 2009, 239–56.

5. M. Lobel, C. J. DeVincent, A. Kaminer, and B. A. Meyer, The Impact of Prenatal Maternal Stress and Optimistic Disposition on Birth Outcomes in Medically High-Risk Women. *Health Psychology* 19, 2000, 544–553; C. K. Rini, C. Dunkel-Schetter, P. D. Wadhwa, and C.A. Sandma, Psychological Adaptation and Birth Out-

comes: The Role of Personal Resources, Stress and Social-Cultural Context in Pregnancy. *Health Psychology* 18, 1999, 333–45.

6. M. F. Scheier, K. A. Matthews, J. F. Owens, et al., Optimism and Rehospitalization Following Coronary Artery Bypass Graft Surgery. *Archives of Internal Medicine* 159, 1999, 829–35.

7. C. Peterson and L. M. Bossio, *Health and Optimism*. New York: Free Press, 1991; M. F. Scheier and C. S. Carver, Dispositional Optimism and Physical Well-Being: the Influence of Generalized Outcome Expectancies on Health. *Journal of Personality and Social Psychology* 55, 1987, 169–210.

8. S. C. Segerstrom and S. E. Sephton, Optimistic Expectancies and Cell-Mediated Immunity: The Role of Positive Affect. *Psychological Science* 21, 2010, 448–55.

9. S. D. Hollon, R. J. DeRubeis, M. D. Evan, M. J. Wiemer, M. J. Garvey, W. M. Grove, and V. B. Tuason, Cognitive Therapy and Pharmacotherapy for Depression: Singly and in Combination. *Archives of General Psychiatry* 49, 1992, 774–781.

10. D. S. Charney, Psychobiological Mechanisms of Resilience and Vulnerability: Implications for Successful Adaptation to Extreme Stress. *American Journal of Psychiatry* 161, 2004, 195–216.

Chapter 3: How to Become an (Even Better) Optimist

1. Positive Thinking: Reduce Stress by Eliminating Negative Self-Talk. www://mayoclinic.com

Chapter 4: The World Is a Better Place Than You Think

1. Manuel Eisner, Long-Term Historical Trends in Violent Crime. *Crime and Justice: A Review of Research* 30, 2003, 83–142; Norbert Elias, *The Civilizing Process: Sociogenetic and Psychogenetic Investigations* (Blackwell, 2000); Charles Kenny, "There Will Not Be Blood," *Optimist* blog, www.foreignpolicy.com, February 6, 2012; Steven Pinker, *The Better Angels of Our Nature: Why Violence Has Declined* (Viking, 2011).

2. United Nations Population Fund, State of the World Population, 2011; Stephen Hawking, *The Universe in a Nutshell* (Bantam, 2001).

3. Ausubel, Jesse H., Peak Farmland and the Prospect for Land Sparing, *Population and Development Review* 38, Suppl. S1, 2013; FAOSTAT, www.faostat.fao.org; Matt Ridley, *The Rational Optimist: How Prosperity Evolves* (Harper Collins, 2010).

4. United Nations, *World Population Ageing* 2009; Kaare Christensen, Gabriele Doblhammer, Roland Rau, and James W Vaupel,

Ageing Populations: The Challenges Ahead, *Lancet*, 374, 2009, 1196–1208.

5. Freedom House, 2012 Freedom in the World; A Glass Half-Full: Representative Government Is Still on the March in Africa, Despite Recent Hiccups, *Economist*, March 12, 2012.

6. Average Annual Hours Actually Worked per Worker; Sangheon Lee, Deirdre McCann, and Jon C. Messenger, *Working Time around the World: Trends in Working Hours, Laws and Policies in a Global Comparative Perspective* (Routledge, 2007); Bureau of Labor Statistics, American Time Use Survey, 2011.

7. Charles Kenney, *Getting Better* (Basic Books, 2011); Daniel Ben-Ami *Ferraris for All* (The Policy Press, 2010); Matt Ridley, *The Rational Optimist* (Harper Collins, 2010); Gregory Clark, *A Farewell to Alms: A Brief Economic History of the World* (Princeton University Press, 2007).

8. Peter H. Diamandis and Steven Kotler, *Abundance: The Future Is Better Than You Think* (Free Press, 2012); Julian Simon, *The Ultimate Resource 2* (Princeton University Press, 1998); "Crowded Out," *Economist*, September 24, 2011.

9. Roland Duong, *Het supermarktparadijs: Gezond kiezen is een kunst*; Rob Lyons, *Panic on a Plate: How Society Developed an Eating Disorder* (Imprint, 2011); E. Scallan, P. M. Griffin, F. J. Angulo, R. V. Tauxe, and R. M. Hoekstra, Foodborne illness Acquired in the United States—Unspecified Agents. *Emerging Infectious Diseases* 17, 2011 (1), 16–22.

10. Adrian Hart, *The Myth of Racist Kids: Anti-racism Policy and the Regulation of School Life* (Manifesto Club, 2009); John McWhorter, Racism in Retreat, *New York Sun*, June 5, 2008; John McWhorter, It Really Is Better Now for Blacks, *The Root*, April 6, 2011; Heather C. West, Prison Inmates at Midyear 2009, statistical tables, Bureau of Justice Statistics, June 23, 2010; Michael J. Rosenfeld, *The Age of Independence: Interracial Unions, Same-Sex Unions, and the Changing American Family* (Harvard University Press, 2007); Robert Jensen, "No Thanks to Thanksgiving," Alternet.org, November 22, 2005; Tom Rodgers: Native American Poverty: A Challenge Too Often Ignored, in *Spotlight on Poverty and Opportunity*. http://www.spotlightonpoverty.org/.

Chapter 5: Welcome to the Age of Optimism

1. https://lentinklab.stanford.edu/welcome/biological_questions.

2. Fred Travis and David Orme-Johnson, Field Model of Consciousness, *International Journal of Neuroscience* 49, 1989, 203–11.

3. http://noosphere.princeton.edu/index.htm.

4. J. S. Hagelin, D. W. Orme-Johnson, M. Rainforth, K. Cavanaugh, C. N. Alexander, S. F. Shatkin, J. L. Davies, A. O. Hughs, E. Ross, Effects of Group Practice of the Transcendental Meditation Program on Preventing Violent Crime in Washington, D.C.: Results of the National Demonstration Project, June–July 1993, Washington, DC, Institute of Science, Technology and Public Policy Technical Report 941 (1994); *Social Indicators Research* 47, 1999 (2), 153–201.

5. Interview with the author, in *Ode*, May/June 2012.

RESOURCES

Baldwin Social Cognition Lab, McGill University, http://baldwinlab.mcgill.ca/labmaterials/materials_BBC.html.

Cousins, Norman. *Anatomy of an Illness* (1985).

Fox, Elaine. *Rainy Brain, Sunny Brain: How to Retrain Your Brain to Overcome Pessimism and Achieve a More Positive Outlook* (2012).

Frankl, Viktor. *Man's Search for Meaning* (1946).

Fredrickson, Barbara L. *Positivity: Top-Notch Research Reveals the 3 to 1 Ratio That Will Change Your Life* (2009).

Gillham, Jane E. (ed.). *The Science of Optimism and Hope* (2000).

Lickerman, Alex. *The Undefeated Mind: On the Science of Constructing an Indestructible Self* (2012).

Paulson, Terry L. *The Optimism Advantage: 50 Simple Truths to Transform Your Attitudes and Actions into Results* (2010).

Peck, M. Scott. *The Road Less Traveled* (1978).

Segerstrom, Suzanne C. *Breaking Murphy's Law: How Optimists Get What They Want from Life—and Pessimists Can Too* (2007).

Seligman, Martin E. P. *Flourish: A Visionary New Understanding of Happiness and Well-Being* (2011).

Seligman, Martin E. P. *Learned Optimism: How to Change Your Mind and Your Life* (1990).

Vaughan, Susan C. *Half Empty Half Full: How to Take Control and Live Life as an Optimist* (2000).

Zander, Benjamin, and Rosamund Stone Zander. *The Art of Possibility* (2000).

ACKNOWLEDGMENTS

THE IMPOSSIBLE JUST TAKES
A LITTLE LONGER

There are many optimists that I need to thank. Over the years I have met with lots of entrepreneurs, writers, inventors, and passionate problem solvers. Some of those conversations led to big stories in *The Intelligent Optimist* (formerly *Ode* magazine). Some were small stories and some were just the beginnings of the next stories. But shared optimism was the thread that tied these conversations together.

On quite a number of occasions I entered such a meeting feeling the burden of running our business and not at all in my most optimistic mind, then left strengthened, freshly inspired after our conversation. That's what optimism does, and in that sense I'm indebted to many people.

My deep special gratitude goes to the team of *The Intelligent Optimist*. Over the years many colleagues who have become friends have contributed to spreading our mission of optimism. "The impossible just takes a little longer," someone once said. That's the core of the optimistic mindset, and *The Intelligent Optimist* team has proven that time and again. A special thank you to Marco Visscher, who contributed much to the thinking and examples in chapter 4.

Chapters 3 and 5 are very much based on the groundbreaking work of psychologist Martin Seligman, who started the sometimes mind-blowing research on optimism many years ago.

My editor at Berrett-Koehler, Jeevan Sivasubramaniam, first jumped enthusiastically on the rough manuscript of this book—which I was happy with—and then led me masterfully to turn it into a much better work that I am now *really* happy with. Everything in between was a fun experience for which I owe him and his team my sincere gratitude.

Finally, whatever I learned and that I share in this book, I learned together with the woman who is the love of my life. We have been together for more than thirty years, and during that long journey we have seen many dreams come true. As you shall see, optimism has everything to do with making dreams come true. And the wonder is that whenever I stumbled she stood. Whenever I fell prey to the always-present forces of pessimism, she helped me see an opening again. Yes, that is love.

Hélène, thank you. Thank you with all my heart.

This is for you.

INDEX

ABOUT THE AUTHOR

© Jordan Lebrecht

In 1995, Jurriaan Kamp left a successful career as the chief economics editor at the leading Dutch newspaper, *NRC Handelsblad*, to found, together with his wife, Hélène de Puy, the "solutions journalism" magazine *Ode* in The Netherlands.

In 2005 Kamp and De Puy moved to California with their four children to launch the international edition of the magazine, renamed *The Intelligent Optimist* in 2012. Under his guidance, the magazine has more than once won the prestigious Maggie Award for journalism.

As both editor-in-chief and CEO of the organization, Kamp has regularly come in ahead of the curve on stories that advance new visions of our world, whether he's advocating a more-is-better approach to sustainability or showcasing thought leaders like alternative health pioneer Johan Boswinkel or Muhammad Yunus, founder of microcredit, long before the mainstream media learns of their work. Kamp wrote his own book about microcredit, *Small Change: How Fifty Dollars Changes the World*.

He has also brought people together through conferences like the Treaty of Noordwijk aan Zee, which laid out the principles of a world economy on a human scale. That theme became the subject of his book *Because People Matter: Building an Economy That Works for Everyone*, published in 2003.

Kamp studied international law at Leyden University. Jurriaan Kamp and Hélène de Puy live in the San Francisco Bay Area.

@JurriaanKamp

facebook.com/jurriaank

Friend me on Google+

Linke with me on Linkedin

www.jurriaankamp.com

ABOUT *THE INTELLIGENT OPTIMIST*

The Intelligent Optimist (formerly *Ode*) is an independent international media platform focused on solutions, possibility, and inspiration. We present optimism as the most effective, efficient, and, by scientific research, confirmed strategy to drive the innovation and creativity that are necessary to solve the problems and meet the challenges that people and society face.

The Intelligent Optimist was founded as *Ode* in 1995 in The Netherlands by Hélène de Puy and Jurriaan Kamp, who left the world of mainstream journalism because of its never-ending focus on whatever goes wrong. Since 2004 the platform is led from twin headquarters in Rotterdam, The Netherlands, and San Francisco.

The Intelligent Optimist publishes a daily selection of solutions-news online, webinars to support the optimism lifestyle, and an award-winning quarterly print magazine in which we point to groundbreaking innovation and the people leading the way. We also offer our readers the chance to connect with these pioneers of possibility and deepen their learning and understanding in interactive online events and courses.

We present intelligent optimism as a way of life because it supports individual and global health and happiness.

Get a free download of our "7 Reasons to Be an Optimist" at theoptimist.com/7reasons.

www.theoptimist.com

Berrett–Koehler
Publishers

Berrett-Koehler is an independent publisher dedicated to an ambitious mission: *Creating a World That Works for All.*

We believe that to truly create a better world, action is needed at all levels—individual, organizational, and societal. At the individual level, our publications help people align their lives with their values and with their aspirations for a better world. At the organizational level, our publications promote progressive leadership and management practices, socially responsible approaches to business, and humane and effective organizations. At the societal level, our publications advance social and economic justice, shared prosperity, sustainability, and new solutions to national and global issues.

A major theme of our publications is "Opening Up New Space." Berrett-Koehler titles challenge conventional thinking, introduce new ideas, and foster positive change. Their common quest is changing the underlying beliefs, mindsets, institutions, and structures that keep generating the same cycles of problems, no matter who our leaders are or what improvement programs we adopt.

We strive to practice what we preach—to operate our publishing company in line with the ideas in our books. At the core of our approach is stewardship, which we define as a deep sense of responsibility to administer the company for the benefit of all of our "stakeholder" groups: authors, customers, employees, investors, service providers, and the communities and environment around us.

We are grateful to the thousands of readers, authors, and other friends of the company who consider themselves to be part of the "BK Community." We hope that you, too, will join us in our mission.

A BK Life Book

This book is part of our BK Life series. BK Life books change people's lives. They help individuals improve their lives in ways that are beneficial for the families, organizations, communities, nations, and world in which they live and work. To find out more, visit **www.bk-life.com**.

Berrett–Koehler
Publishers

A community dedicated to creating
a world that works for all

Dear Reader,

Thank you for picking up this book and joining our worldwide community of Berrett-Koehler readers. We share ideas that bring positive change into people's lives, organizations, and society.

To welcome you, we'd like to offer you a free ebook. You can pick from among twelve of our bestselling books by entering the promotional code **BKP92E** here: http://www.bkconnection.com/welcome.

When you claim your free ebook, we'll also send you a copy of our e-newsletter, the *BK Communiqué*. Although you're free to unsubscribe, there are many benefits to sticking around. In every issue of our newsletter you'll find

- A free ebook
- Tips from famous authors
- Discounts on spotlight titles
- Hilarious insider publishing news
- A chance to win a prize for answering a riddle

Best of all, our readers tell us, "Your newsletter is the only one I actually read." So claim your gift today, and please stay in touch!

Sincerely,

Charlotte Ashlock
Steward of the BK Website

Questions? Comments? Contact me at bkcommunity@bkpub.com.

Certified

Corporation
bcorporation.net